Copyright © Jonatha

First published 2009

This edition 2013

No part of this publication may be reproduced, transmitted or stored in a retrieval system without prior permission from the publisher, nor may it be circulated in any binding other than that in which it is published.

This book is dedicated to; my wife Jill and our handsome sons Connor and Michael who have put up with my disappearances for years, also to my wider family for their continued support in the face of what seemed like madness.

Acknowledgements

Cover Photo: used by kind permission of "Amosnet.de."

All managers and staff I have worked with. You included the best of the best and the worst of the worst.

To 'Steve' and 'Jill' a big thank you for making my time away a little more bearable.

"Having been a consultant and a manager most of my professional life, I couldn't help but smile and giggle as I was going through Jonathan's stories "aggravations, idiocy, mediocrity and absolute lunacy" that you get to deal with in the field. Living out of your suitcase, "job" in one city, family in another...having a phone relationship with your children while dealing with the client organization's self-inflicted problems -- that is something that a lot of consultants / interim managers can relate to.

Besides the "war stories" (delivered in a light-hearted, almost "folksy" style), and attacking some stereotypes about management, Jonathan provides a number of tips and concepts that may mean a difference between surviving in the management job or failing at it.

"Unfortunately in most places I've worked, when someone becomes a manager they think they just need to do their existing job but better."

So dang true...

Alex Makarski
Project Turnaround Specialist
www.alexmakarski.com
Richmond Hills, Toronto, Canada,

Acknowledgements	3
It's all about me	8
The deal – working with agencies.	15
The client	18
The Consultants lifestyle	24
The racist night out	44
Final thoughts	62
Collection of thoughts on management	65
Professional managing skills	65
The art of Management	67
A Good Director	67
Delegation v Organisation	68
Legitimacy and trust	74
Working out who is who	81
Communication & language	91
Hypnotic words	95
Dextifing	96
Consultant as a crutch	115
Cleaning up mess	120
Problem processes	122
Building a process map	123
Problem People	126
A successful organisation?	128
Expenses	145
Working for the council	158
Anyone can work for me…	167
Do I care for staff uniform?	169
Keeping a distance	171
What does being off sick actually mean?	183
Failure Demand & motivation	194
Disaster recovery	201
To be a 'Chartered Manager'	205

What I am doing now. 207
Do you get it?..210
Further reading...212

Why & how?
Before I start, I think should tell you why I wrote this book and what sort of things you can expect from "The confessions of an interim manager".
The idea of the book came from the experiences I have had, some funny some sad, some quite oddball and some you wouldn't believe, during my working life as a travelling consultant on the road.
I wanted to show, you the reader, that all that glitters is not gold, while at the same time helping those who have responsibility for/over others, in various situations, to be better managers with a bit more understanding.

What will you get from this book?
Within these pages I have put hints and tips, methodologies and strategies, examples and stories to encourage you to improve your management style with none of the boring stuff you learn on training courses.

Included with these things are my own thoughts and feelings about what it's like living out of a suitcase miles away from home and doing a demanding (but highly paid) job.

You will find that I mention many colleagues, staff, directors and managers who have taught me many things.

These people have padded out the training I received while doing my B.A. degree in management and I feel that now I can speak with some degree of confidence about the issues related in this book.

I am not going to dish the dirt and reveal my true feelings about the people I have written about, although the offer from a certain Sunday paper was tempting…

I am not going to name names and describe places, but if you have ever worked with me you will be able to recognise yourself so be careful who you show this too as they may recognise you too…

I would especially like to pay tribute to the following people:
My wife and family
"Steve"- who is probably the best manager I have ever worked with and a thoroughly decent bloke.

I have divided this book into two sections.

The first is concerned with the lifestyle of a consultant: the events, happenings and goings on that are not always (certainly not in mine) in the consultants' sales brochure.

The second part talks about management skills: – a mixture of skills and techniques that I have used, in various places to get things done.

Please feel free to add them to your own management tool box.

It's all about me

At the time of the events in this book, I was in my mid 30's; married (which I still am) and my children were 3 and 5 years old.

In the 1990's before I had the responsibilities of family I drifted into a job with a small local authority after leaving college with a B.A. degree.

I was put into Housing Benefit. I will not talk much about the technical aspect of this apart from making you aware that:

Housing Benefit customers are among the most vulnerable in society. They include the elderly, the disabled, lone parents and the long term unemployed.

Working with these client groups doubles the problems of working for the council. You are also fair game for all sorts of pressure groups as diverse as women's refuge to the Citizens Advice Bureau and from Housing Associations to local law centres.

Working in the Housing Benefits arena is not a normal office job and often needs social/interpersonal skills and administrative knowledge, far beyond that of the normal office job, to be carried out effectively.

It is an expensive and complicated business. Most Local Authorities will spend 20% – 30% of their budgets on housing benefits and it has been called un-administrable by some.

From 1991 -1998 I graduated from office clerk to Senior Officer/Assistant Manager and during this time several changes impacted on how Housing Benefit was administrated.

Local Authorities had always been pretty much unregulated and performance management was for "city whiz kids". But a change in 1993 saw the abolition of the Community Charge and the job settled down.

It was the era in which computers were coming to the fore and "Microsoft Windows" was moving every thing forward. The world was expanding (although not yet online) and I could see where it was going and also that I wasn't going there with my current employer.

(Incidentally, the first training session I ever led was to show people how to cut and paste in Windows 3.1)

I began looking around for other jobs and found it was quite difficult. Housing Benefit was all I knew and with only 450 local authorities in the country there were really only 450, immediately possible, job options.

In my workplace nothing seemed exciting or seemed to stretch me and I was surrounded by indifferent managers and unmotivated, miserable people (who if they had worked for me, wouldn't have worked for me very long). I went to work each day feeling frustrated that I might have to stay where I was after all.

I was cycling to work two, sometimes three days a week. It was a journey of about nine miles (15 kilometres) each way, and it meant that every morning I had to get into my cycling gear, on arrival at work get out of it again and then get into appropriate clothing for working in.

The cycling was no bad thing really as I was a wannabe triathlete and it was a good opportunity to get some training in.

What was awkward and became a particular thorn in the side, was getting changed at work.

There were two of three of us who cycled to work and we all had the same problem of finding somewhere to get changed but no-one was interested in helping us sort out a regular changing area or room, for just 10 minutes use, twice a day.

The disregard given to cyclists by the authority was shown on one particular occasion when it turned out that I was the only one who had come to work on my bike that day. When it came to leave again for home I found that my clothes and possessions had been locked in a room, without my knowledge, and nobody seemed able to sort it out.

It was a different story however, when the management sent for me to change into my gear because some 'green' publicity was needed.

This I thought was not the way I would motivate someone... although it did in fact increase my motivation for getting out of there.

The straw that finally broke the camels back though, was when my application to cover for the office manager (who wanted maternity leave) was disallowed on my behalf without my knowledge.

I was starting to lose interest in the job that I was doing, I felt I was being used by some and ignored by others. The only thing that seemed of any interest was managing the constant changes in Housing Benefits being made by Government.

Government regulations are changed at least every six months and training for the administration of Housing Benefit is a constant requirement because of this.
More often than not external visitors would turn up at the offices and deliver this training and after watching and talking to them I thought to myself "I could do that!" so I did.

I approached a couple of training agencies for information and found out that - agencies secured a booking with a Local Authority and charged them a daily rate for someone to come in and do some training. Even better, they wrote the training course and paid for all the printing and stationary.

I wasn't yet ready to leave the job I was in, after all I had a family to feed, but it seemed like a good idea to book a day off from work and spend it training staff in another authority. This had the double bonus of gaining experience and earning a few extra quid as well.

Finally after a couple of years of booking days off I had gained a lot of experience working with various businesses and quite a good reputation as a trainer.

I was in regular contact with a friend who was a managing consultant for a manufacturing consultancy and a good sounding post for ideas.

At the time management consultancy was a field of expertise I didn't know much about but it didn't take me long to learn that in general terms a consultant is higher up the food chain than a trainer.

This is because (in very general terms), a consultant will be on site to diagnose problems AND THEN seek the services of a training professional.

So after a considerable amount of discussion with the wife I made a big leap of faith, handed my notice in at work and set out to be a management consultant.

(There I was, suddenly I'm a consultant, when only a week before I couldn't even spell it!)

What coloured my landscape?
How could a mere trainer suddenly become a highly paid consultant you ask?

You will be able to tell as you learn about my style of doing things that I like to take into account the wider environment and how that affects everything I might do, so I made sure that my leap into consultancy was not going to be straight into a deep hole.

In 2003-4 the Department of Work and Pensions (the Government department responsible for Housing Benefit), implemented a 'Help' fund of £200,000 to be spent throughout 2003 – 2006, to pay for sustainable projects which would result in improved department performance.

This fund money couldn't be spent on anything like staff overtime, because that by itself would not sustain improvement, but it could be used to fund external agency staff to back up internal staff so they could then go off and learn new skills or cover a different job or project.

Of course with all this money washing around loads of companies and consultancies sprang up selling everything from CD ROM tool kits to 'health checks' by armies of consultants who would descend (blue lights flashing) to clean the wounds of a troubled service.

For large PLC's supplying local government it was, (hopefully without being libellous), a case of "we will have some of that and think of something to sell you in a little while"

The 'hole' which I did in fact enter was actually being slowly filled with many different types of consultants, interim consultants and managers all of whom had been "Help" funded.

During my first year, I was involved, at one particular site, with an initial meeting about a particular project that was to be set up – and during the ten minute 'around the table' introduction, it revealed interims who were Chief Accountants, Payroll Managers, and Exchequer Managers etc.

"Blimey," I thought "in the past temps and contractors were brought in to clean the toilets and mop up the floor now we are running the place"

The deal – working with agencies.

It may seem that I just slotted in to the interim consultant/ manger business like a round peg in a round hole. The 'help fund' had encouraged many management agencies to start upon the business of recruiting potential interim managers and all manner of temporary workers. They did this in very different ways and it was important to me that I find the right agencies to work with and for.

I sent my CV to a couple of 'promising' agencies and waited for their call.

How the 'deal' tended to work was that consultancy firms/agencies generally had a high profile in the world of local government.

They would find and secure a placement in a local authority and then start the search for a suitable consultant, from either their own employees (PAYE) or freelancers like me, to fill it.

The way it worked with me was that they would ring, see if I was available for the dates and the post they had found. I would then invoice the agency for my time (and agreed expenses) and they in turn would invoice the client/council for more, thus making a profit from my work.

In truth, it was a mutually beneficial arrangement. I didn't have the resources to advertise in the Local Government Chronicle newspaper or sponsor an award at a black tie dinner, and with no other job to fall back on I didn't have the time to look for placements myself.

It must be said however that agencies were not in it to help you out; they were in it for themselves. If I couldn't do the dates they wanted or asked for greater expenses due to distances covered etc. they could always find another interim to do the job. Agencies do not preach or expect loyalty and this dog eat dog – devil may care – attitude was good while it lasted but not something a married man with children could build a career on.

Sometimes the circumstances leading up to a placement were quite rushed and at other times very slow. This would usually depend on the prevarication of the client and quite often they didn't know what was best for them or what they really wanted.

I could generally tell how close the agency had got to getting a placement was by the language and the tone of voice of the marketing recruitment consultant down the phone.

A conversation which included a passing the time of day talking about football, cricket the weather etc. usually signified a sounding out, to see if I was busy or going to be busy in the future, but when a job or placement had been agreed to or needed filling immediately their tone was sharper and much more abrupt.

Watching your back
How well you got on with the agencies or consultancy firms depended on how closely you had to watch your own back. The marketing recruitment consultant at one firm would regularly say after agreement on a placement

"If there's anything you need or anything I can do to help, just ring and let me know" and other general patter and waffle.

Whenever he said it, I felt sure that he didn't really mean it and on the one occasion that I did ask

"Can you get me a duplicate timesheet?"

He replied:

"I can't actually do that; can you ring such a body?"

and because of my relative inexperience I would spend time ringing around to find someone to get me a timesheet, or whatever it was that he couldn't help me with.

Then I realized it wasn't very professional to be seen sorting out such 'trivial' matters myself especially when I was supposed to be in charge of the office.

As in all offices it was something of an open secret that consultants and interims were well paid and thus not a smart thing to do to draw attention to this fact by speaking openly on the phone about it.

I soon learnt to be a little pushier and said, " Sorry but I'm here to serve the client, can you please arrange to have one sent to me because we have a lot of problems here and I haven't got time to chase up time sheets".

Then as if by magic! Someone would provide a duplicate timesheet

Checking out the website first
Whenever I was offered a placement one of the first things I did was to look at the website of the authority concerned.
Some local authorities had very good interactive websites and as I looked at them I felt a lifting of spirits at the thought of going there. Others, although up to date enough to have a website, seemed to be stuck in the past.

The client

Although the money is good - the real point of being an interim manager/ consultant is to help out the service or client you have been assigned to. Sometimes these were in complete disarray and barely managing to stay afloat and serve customers.

"Helping' the client can often mean a number of things. Sometimes you are given the sketchiest of briefings from your agency. The placing of consultants/interims can be a highly competitive market and a firm will often place the consultant and sort out the details afterwards.

Once or twice, I turned up on the first day and the client, knowing the 'game' asked "So what do you think you are here for?" and then proceeded to tell me what they thought they needed and why I was there.

This might not have been what was in the 'brief' I had been given but 'the customer is always right" aren't they?

Sometimes the need was, to help some staff on an individual basis. A busy office always meant there was a backlog of work or bottle neck in the system somewhere to sort out.

My work in that situation therefore was to spot those who had problems, listen to them, and find a solution.

In lots of cases staff just needed to moan at someone in authority for a while, and it was important for me to find out if this moaning masked a real problem or just general discontent from the staff.

Arriving at one placement, it was clear that two managers were striving to hold their service together in the face of many difficulties.

At the initial meeting I had with them (lasting over 2 hours) it was the managers who did most of the talking. It was quite clear that they were ready to unload all their troubles and just listening to them was enough to earn my fee for that day.

>TIP - When people start to repeat themselves it is a sign to move the conversation on. A sentence to summarise and close like "Well that's enough talking lets do some doing" will usually move the conversation along.

But it wasn't just about listening to the client, their staff and their problems sometimes I would actually have to do something...

Occasionally a client would ask me to take on some sort of project which they obviously didn't have time to do and in general I was happy to do this.

However, at one particular business the project I had been asked to take on was really against my better judgment and was obviously something that the client didn't want to touch with a barge pole, but it had to be done anyway.

If I had been in their position and not actually an interim working for them I wouldn't have touched it either.

So what did I do?
Well, I was there to do the job regardless of my own feelings about it and obviously if I had refused to do it I would have not been paid so I went ahead with it.

As an independent contractor I did of course have own reputation to think of. Being tagged with working on a failed project could have really hurt my reputation. I knew that I would have to be very careful and keep records of everything that I did and how and why I did it, so that any backlash would be avoided.

It was obvious to me at the time that this project was a real non starter, but I wasn't there to be a whistle blower I was there to do a job.

A year or two later, I was asked to return to do another stint of work there. The project I had worked on previously was mentioned only in hushed tones as though speaking of the dead!

My management style
The authoritarian management style of the private sector which focuses on targets, performance management and outputs, was and still is in places, in its infancy in the public sector where such a strict style doesn't go down very well.

During my time as an interim I came in contact with and worked with quite a few people who seemed not to have grasped that the days when the public called you 'Sir', because you worked at the council, were gone.

If you like watching repeats of 1970's-80's drama on TV you will see the 'man from the council' turn up in a three piece suit and knock at the door of some humble women dressed in an apron and wearing curlers.

Nowadays, they will probably turn up in casual trousers and an open necked shirt! The woman in apron and curlers might still be around in some areas however.

I suppose that because of the type of person I am - neither the straight laced 'suit' nor the 'open necked shirt' but rather a bit of both I dressed appropriately regarding the situation I needed to deal with.

As my experience grew, I developed a 'get along' management style This was in line with my preference to be in among people, helping them to do a good job by working with and supporting them, while at the same time expecting them to do what is required for the job.

I can illustrate this by talking about football. England football matches have become something of a strange event for the business world in the last 10 years or so. For some reason half the country expects to come to a halt and automatically get time off work.

Depending on where the World Cup/European Championship is being held leads to a wholesale 'downing of tools', and requests for annual leave and more flexi time.

If you are going to be short staffed then some people are going to be disappointed when you say "No" when they ask for time off.

However you too can become hypnotised by the hype, but it is essential that you don't relent and grant leave when you otherwise wouldn't.
Normal rules should always apply because
1. Not every one is likely to be interested in football.
2. Not everyone (Including customers) will want to watch.
3. Not everyone supports England.

In one particular place, trying to be flexible, I arranged for a portable TV set to be brought into the office allowing those who wanted to 'watch' the match 'live' to do so while they worked. However the sound had to be turned off – we don't want every one to think that council workers spend their time watching TV….

Having said that, when you read further on, based on some of the things I say, you will probably think that I am some sort of ogre who likes making trouble and annoying people just for the sake of it.

Not true, if you work for me and you come to work on time, do what you are supposed to do and then go home, we will get along like a house on fire. I will make it my mission to make you happy in your work and will rock boats and bend rules to get what is best for you and the rest of the team.

In fact, if you go for a drink on Friday lunch times, then I might even come with you just to buy you a drink.

On the other hand, if you are repeatedly late, don't do what you are supposed to do, prat about, generally loaf around, make a cock up and try to cover it up or not tell me, then we will fall out…

The Consultants lifestyle

Until I actually became a consultant I supposed like everyone else that they were men in their mid 50's driving around in big cars, wearing expensive suits, having a permanent suntan and a slight beer belly, along with plenty of time to go off and play golf. Although some of this might be true there is a bit more to it than that.

I found that while consultants are 'shopped for' and even head hunted by agencies they can be shunted around like freight from one business/authority to another and although they can look smart and prosperous they are to all intents and purposes living out of suitcases. Large cars are often just a way to travel, in comfort, the hundred's of miles from family homes to placements.

Working so far away means overnight stays in various hotels, B&B'S and farmhouses.

Going to sleep in a strange bed can have the side effects of an uncomfortable night and the tendency to wake up very early.

After tossing and turning all night, I've lost count of the number of times I've got up and read the paper or a book until it seemed a reasonable time to get up.

As a consequence the days become very long. Waking up at half past 5 or quarter to 6 in the morning, having to work all day, and then travel for two or more hours to get home or go back to the same hotel and that 'wonderful' bed.

After travelling back home at the weekends and finally getting two good nights of sleep it makes it all the harder to have to pack up and start again. One of the things my wife could never understand is that when you have to get up early to leave on Monday mornings, you can't just have an easy end to the weekend sitting and watching TV, you have to prepare everything on Sunday night for the next week.

This becomes very mentally tiring. You have to constantly think in advance, often three or four days in advance, about the things you will need:
Have I got enough shirts, pants, socks and shaving stuff?
Have I got enough paperwork for things that I might have done or need to be doing?
Have I got something on my computer from a previous placement that could help me?

I would try to get all this done and ready so that I could walk straight out of the front door. Unfortunately there was many a time when I have had to go back up stairs again to look for a belt, a tie or some shoes and disturbed the wife or the children.
Note – My first summer holiday after the start of my work as a consultant was spent, not in Lanzarote or southern Spain as you might be thinking but in southern England – Cornwall in fact. We were not even in a hotel but camping and it did nothing but rain!

Effect on "normal" family life

It's a sad fact of life that no one really cares about your family life except you. The client doesn't care – because they don't know you and the consultancy firm don't care – because they can't earn from it.

So the consultant is left with their personal feelings and has to deal with them as best they can.

I tend to be quite emotional at times, especially about my children as you will see and I had not yet hardened myself to being away for so long. They were both still very young and I didn't want to miss out on then growing up.

It was November and I was in a placement miles away from home. My youngest son had started school in the September of that particular year. I was aware that I was under some pressure to perform at this placement, although this was never communicated to me directly, because of the failures of previous consultants supplied by the same agency and I had a strong suspicion that having a day off so soon into the contract was not the way to show willing.

When I arrived home one weekend early in the project, there was a letter telling me that my little boy had been chosen to play Joseph in the school nativity production, which just happened to be taking place on my birthday.

This was his first year at school and it was happening on my birthday and there was no way I could see it because I would have to be at the placement.

OK so he would only be walking on to the stage dressed in an old sheet and a tea towel round his head - but he was Joseph, on my birthday and I was two and a half hours away in a hotel by myself.

I couldn't help myself, I cried for two hours because I would miss it.

When I went to pay for my evening meal that birthday night the receptionist said "There is a card for you." She handed it to me; it was a birthday card from my parents, sent directly to the Hotel. Happy birthday to me!

The following year I was still working away from home and living in hotels and it had started to become easier to leave house and home every Monday morning in fact it had become normal.

My children were now six and four and had started to bring some of their work home from school/nursery to show us what they had been doing.

My eldest son had drawn a picture of a cat and had written underneath it 'clever cat Connor '

I can see the picture now, then he said "Daddy, will you take it to put at the side of your desk" and I said that I would and put it on top of the suitcase to take down with me.

When I finally arrived at the placement I opened the boot of the car to get out my briefcase and the picture was there staring up at me. After spending some time back in the car I wiped my face and went to work.

The picture never made it to my desk because I knew it would make me cry every time I looked at it.

So much for the 'hard man' at work!
Lost and out of control

I used to ring home every evening after work when I returned to the hotel or B&B to check if everything was OK at home. This tended to be around 6-6:30pm. Sometimes there would be no answer because I had forgotten they were out somewhere but one particular night stands out.

No answer at 6:00pm – try later.

No answer at 6:30pm – OK maybe they have walked down to the village shops.

Went off swimming & rang again at 8:00pm – No answer.

Hmmm – There is a limit to what a woman can do with two children under ten at tea time and without a car. So I started ringing round immediate family asking if they might have seen her or perhaps taken her and the kids out.

No – no sign all day.

8:30pm– Still no answer – (Tried mobile - switched off obviously)

9:00pm – Getting worried now. I rang my sister. The panic in my voice obviously moved her and she very kindly offered to nip over to our house to investigate.

9:15pm – My phone rings. "It's me" says a familiar voice…

"Where are you?" in an annoyed but relieved manner.

"At home"

"Where have you been all night?" angrier tone – how dare she be so calm when I've been out of my mind for the last three hours!

"At home"

"Where are the lads?" (She's done something to them!)

"In bed fast asleep"

"Where is the phone?" (Do you think I'm stupid?)

Sounds of movement down the earpiece (obviously looking around)

"Oh – It's off the hook sorry…have you been worried?"

"Err, just a little…" said through gritted teeth

And that's the root of it. When you are 2 hours away from home it might as well be 200 hours. The feeling of being out of control can be very worrying and stressful.

Hotel living
When you are working miles away and missing your family where are you expected to lay your tired and weary and lonely body at night?

In the beginning…when the agencies were splashing in the fountain of 'help fund' money your tired, weary body would be allowed to experience the wonders of an expensive hotel at the end of a long day.

Some agencies would usually have someone whose job was to look for accommodation for the interims under their banner. As money was seen to be no object, a hotel, was the preferred, and in some cases the nearest and easiest choice.

So there I was staying in hotels, sometimes with three or four other interims. The hotels were part of one of the large international chains (with a glossy website written in five or six European languages) and I remember, the first time I stayed in one.

From the car park I crunched up the long gravel driveway to the hotel. Suitcase in one hand my laptop in the other, I thought this was very high brow and not the type of place I would normally stay at.

OK, I knew about these places, I'd been to a couple of courses in smart hotel conference rooms, but I still felt a little intimidated walking through the glass and gilt doors and after traversing across the marble floor to the reception area I was quite overwhelmed by the efficiency of the attractive young lady who took my booking details.

Quite obviously to her, if I was staying in a hotel like this one, I must have been a well travelled businessman used to this sort of lifestyle. Through my eyes I felt like a country yokel on his first visit to the big city.

My room was an executive room with a large leather armchair and a large window which looked out over leafy gardens. There was a large bath with complimentary bathrobes, it was all so ......large!

Of course I partook of all this opulence and had a shower, got dried in a thick white towel and got ready to go and find something to eat.

After looking at the restaurant menu it was obviously very much out of my price range. I had no idea of how much spending was permitted for my subsistence so I just had a bar snack. This was to be my routine for the first few nights of my stay in the grand hotel and because of this I remember feeling very hungry during my first days at this placement.

I was too scared and too new to the consultant's lifestyle to 'splash out' at the restaurant – I knew I was allowed breakfast but to play safe this was followed by a 'take away' sandwich at lunchtime, then I had nothing to eat until the bar snack (usually burger and chips) in the hotel at 8pm.

It dawned on me then, that I would need to buy or bring with me everything I wanted. There was no cupboard in my room full of the usual staples like coffee, tea and biscuits and no kettle to turn on. After all wasn't that what room service was for? The tiring feeling of having to think in advance was back.

I suppose in the back of my head I was thinking that people would assume that I was "Lording" it up eating and drinking at the expense of the client.

People on a household budget like mine don't generally get to stay in posh hotels unless they are on holiday. Living a hotel lifestyle at the expense of someone else is to me objectionable and consultant or not I couldn't change that.

I decided that the secret was not to be lavish, to boast or to draw attention to my expenses claims. As my experience of hotels grew, through the placements I was given in different areas of the country. Not all of them were as lavish as in the beginning and I became more confident in what I could and couldn't allow myself to spend but even so, when it came to the end of each week/month and the time of reckoning – getting the expenses/time sheet signed was a ticklish moment.

After all I was asking the client to confirm that they were happy with my work, that what I had spent was justifiable, and hopefully they would pay me.

I once presented my expenses sheet to a particular director who was acutely aware of how much he was paying for me. He studied the sheet very closely for a few moments (which seemed like ten minutes) he got out his calculator and checked a few things then finally he looked up and said "I can't sign this".

A heart stopping moment: then
"Is there a problem?" I asked.
He said "There's only one L in Bollinger" and smiled.

Yes, he had a sense of humour and he had just made me acutely aware that he was in control.

I was learning that the bottom line was you had to account for every last penny on your expenses sheet or you paid for everything you consumed yourself

Pushed together

Because agencies usually had interim workers on their books that were working in and around the same authorities they would put some of them in the same hotels or in other hotels near by.

A side effect of living away from home is that you meet similar people doing the same thing. You are drawn together every day over breakfast, evening meal or just a cup of coffee.

You may be from a different part of the country have different social backgrounds, interests and hobbies with nothing else in common except work. Your conversation will always revolve around and revert back to work or associated themes such as hotels, traffic problems etc

This has the spin off benefit of developing networking and social conversation skills.

An incident I remember very well occurred when I went to pay for a meal in a restaurant and a photograph of my children fell on the floor I picked it up and passed it to my colleague and said "they are my boys" to which she replied that "they are little rascals aren't they" and passed it straight back.. I didn't expect her to gush over them but I felt as though she had "blanked" me.

The next time we met she had a large bundle of photographs showing a horse event with her and the horses. I have no interest in horses and felt no compelling reason why I should spend time looking at all her photographs. However in the interests of harmony I tried to look interested.

In general however, meeting and interacting with others made quite a difference to my life as an interim because it wasn't just me having these experiences there was someone to talk to, and in some cases the people I met in this artificial situation became friends.

Pretty soon - my romance with the hotel started to fizzle out a bit, simple things like the TV not working, or it being set to an incomprehensible satellite channel, the bath and shower water being generally cold, or so hot that you couldn't stand it, all put together they become very irritating.

Apart from those little inconveniences I was fully aware that I was living with other people, strangers, whose lives meant nothing to me...
I was intimately connected to them at breakfast or dinner and had to make polite conversation and finally when I went to bed they would stand outside my room in the early hours discussing noisily about their day and what they were going to do tomorrow and who with.

Then there were the fire alarms – with the risk of fire ever present most hotel alarms are hyper-sensitive. Sometimes so sensitive, that they will go off because of kettle/bath steam, cigarette smoke when a smoker's door is opened, aerosol sprays, and you name it.

As a result I have lost count of the number of times I have been woken in the middle of the night/early morning, to stand outside for 30-40 minutes.

To brighten things up for us (although I'm sure they didn't meant to) the hotel occasionally set challenges, especially in the billing department.

My fee was all inclusive and because of this, instead of using money in the hotel you were given a 'card'. This did it all; room service, bar, restaurant, room charge and you didn't have to pay until you checked out, at which time the receptionist 'swiped' the card and you paid the bill.

Being aware that my expenses would be examined, I always looked at and checked over the receipt.

Sorting out some of the problems that those little pieces of plastic made, would have foxed an accountant – on different occasions I was charged for: someone else's room, items I hadn't used such as pornographic films, support services and newspapers etc. and to top it all I would sometimes have the meals I had eaten the week before or even another persons meal on the receipt. Trying to track down the original receipts would have done Sherlock proud.
Having seen the catastrophes that were being made on my bill receipts other colleagues were checking theirs a little more. I soon found that reception wasn't just challenging me; a colleague of mine

'Jill' was also having trouble with her receipts and reception in general.

In effect the trouble with her bill receipts wasn't that they were adding things on but were missing things off. Being the honest person that she is, she took her receipt back to the receptionist and pointed out to the lady there that there was no evening meal on the bill.

You would think that the receptionist would be pleased to be able to easily account for unbalanced tills at the end of the day but 'Jill' was quite taken aback when the bill was snatched out of her hand and with a loud 'tut' the receptionist banged hard on the keyboard to illustrate her displeasure. Why?

Simply because there was a queue at the desk and this extra query meant that she had to do some more work.

Hmmm – I didn't see that variety of customer services on their latest advert.

These 'rays of brightness' were just another nail in the coffin of my initial hotel fantasies, familiarity was starting to breed contempt, not only at the reception desk but in the rooms the service and especially the food department.

After all hotel food is hotel food. When you first look at it you think "That looks nice" then you eat it and it is, but only for so long.

The novelty of a cooked breakfast (cooked by someone else and no washing up) was too good to resist at the beginning and being paid 'all inclusive' meant that I could have a full cooked breakfast (or the big dipper) every day if I felt like it.

This was good in that it allowed me to live the ideal life as seen in the adverts. There were no feelings of hunger at 10.15a.m, or the need to nip off for a break.

However I soon realized that hotel 'Full English' breakfasts were not necessarily cooked fresh every morning but sometimes left to 'warm' (maybe even overnight).

Apart from the obvious food, health and hygiene considerations, there was the struggling with containers which didn't always open, the spraying of the juice or milk as it was poured over myself or someone else, the crispiness (or not) of the cornflakes, breakfast became a very risky business and the excitement soon wore off.

To have an English breakfast cooked to order was obviously preferable to the buffet type breakfast, but then there was always the worry that I would be late for work if I wasn't served promptly.

The menu at a hotel is fine for the one off visit where you can have a choice of a variety of meals from what seems to be a varied menu, but when you are staying there the menu - although changed every day, is of course the same for the week after and the week after that and so on.... It soon loses its novelty and you see through the flowery descriptions

We had been in the same hotel for about three weeks and it was becoming easy to see that it wasn't just me that was becoming disillusioned with the hotels.

A colleague actually coined the phrase 'Hotel sickness.' and explained it thus:

'All the rooms are the same, all the décor is the same, have I been here before? Wasn't I in this room last week? Didn't I have this meal last week? Why have they taken my straight jacket away?

Without any way reason for getting out, looking at four walls from early evening onwards for nights on end can drive you mad.

It was a relief sometimes to be moved on to other hotels once a job had finished. At least the view was changed if not the corporate decor.

Working with a couple of other consultants we were lucky enough to be placed in a well to do southern UK town which had, along its main streets and alley ways, lots of restaurants all brightly lit serving food from all over the world. What could have been more tempting?

So to relieve the boredom of hotel food and eating in the formal restaurant atmosphere we invented "International Night".

We started out by accident at the curry shop after a power cut at the hotel. This made such a palatable change that soon, in fact, every Tuesday night we went to a restaurant serving food from a different country, from Mexican, Italian, Chinese, Thai, and South African, even the English restaurant counted.

We got so excited about this that we even spoke about trimming up the office with flags and bunting – in the style of the World Cup or Olympics – to celebrate that one night of the week.

At another placement, my friend and colleague ''Steve'' and I were increasingly fed up with the staple hotel meal and the stale hotel air, and decided to go to the Pub across the road from the hotel for an occasional evening meal.

One night we had a special treat as we had a couple of consultant colleagues with us and friends of friends who had agreed to meet up for dinner.

In total there were 7 of us

This pub was no exception to the British disease of being short staffed and was constantly at stretching point.

It was a pub whose staple customers seemed to be young to middle aged couples without children. Our 'rent a crowd' of consultants caused some disruption to normal service. It wasn't just that suddenly there was a gang of several people invading the premises, the fact that we all insisted on paying for separate meals because of our individual expense accounts that caused chaos and more disruption

We knew that there was no way all of us could be served at the same time and so did the landlord, so to ease the delay the he came over to pass the time of day.

The evening itself was very successful and apart from the rumpus at the start we all had a pleasant time with no other incidents

It was almost a week after the group expedition; all the visiting consultants had left for other sites so we decided to give the hotel menu a miss again and went to the pub.

The pub was busy but the landlord came over to us again and started to chat and it was as if the week had never passed. The conversation was as if it were like playing the same record.

"Are you by yourselves this time? Where's the rest of your gang? Staying at the hotel are you?"
"Yes, we're working for the local council"
"Oh yes, doing what?"

"Oh boring stuff really, you wouldn't want to know"
"I didn't think they had any money!"
"That's not really our concern"
"Well they're always pleading poverty in the papers, so they must have if they can pay for you two to lord it up in here"
"We are not from round here so we wouldn't know".
"Where are you from?"
"(Yawn) Sheffield"
"Oh right, The Full Monty - can you do it? – my wife's cousin is from Sheffield"
"Oh really. Where abouts?"
"I don't know it's a steep road and that bloke used to live next door, tell me some famous people from Sheffield"
"Michael Palin, Def Leopard, Human League, Joe Cocker, Michael Vaughan, Brendan Ingle."
"No it's none of them; anyway I'll not disturb you boys any longer. Do you want to see the menu?"
"Yes please" (but I suppose it hasn't changed since last week)

Although his politeness was very laudable, after all he didn't have to come and talk to us - it did get a bit tiresome after the third or fourth week and I think he gave up eventually

The phrase "where's the rest of the gang" did however become a bit of a catchphrase for us.

That pub featured quite centrally during my time at that work site. Although I frequented it for evening meals with "Steve" I could also be seen there occasionally at an earlier time after work with an in house member of staff who lived locally and I went swimming with. I could leave the car, go swimming, have a drink and a chat with the member of staff, and then change for the evening meal.

To go in with a 'local person' and have a beer, then return an hour or so later to eat, really confused the landlord, he wasn't sure which record to play and when.

It wasn't always so hard to try to keep the conversation moving along however.

The racist night out

Before I tell this next story though, I will tell you of the main players on this particular evening.

They were; my colleague 'Steve', our previous colleague "Louise',' who was now working at a site nearly 20 miles away and me.

After a phone call from 'Louise' earlier that day 'Steve' and I agreed to meet her at 7.30 to eat at 8pm. We all knew the Restaurant, it was quite posh and a few miles away situated at the edge of a river in a beautiful countryside setting. 'Louise' had also explained that she was bringing one of her colleagues ('Debbie') with her and did we mind.

'Debbie' was an accountancy consultant at the site she was working at.

So it was to be the four of us.

At the restaurant 'Louise' and 'Debbie' turned up along with another man who, suffice to say, did not look like a consultant. In fact 'Debbie' had brought along her husband ('Dave').

Unlike other consultants, 'Debbie' and 'Dave' had not booked into hotel or B&B, they had rented a house. They lived in the house during the week and went home at the weekends.

I thought that this was quite an odd thing to do, even allowing for the fact that Debbie was an accountant and a consultant, which was likely to be double the oddball factor. A quick glance from 'Steve' showed that he thought so too.

'Debbie' was clearly a smart and attractive lady and as an accountancy consultant obviously good at her job, when we asked 'Dave' what he did while she was working on site, he said that he rode his motor bike round the country lanes, went into the local William Hill or Ladbrokes and liked to watch "At the Races" a satellite TV horse racing channel, in the afternoons.

Small talk later revealed that 'Dave' would have been starting a Microsoft IT course at the local college but had not got round to enrolling and so currently he was not on a course and without a job.

Conversation was general but starting to feel a bit edgy and gradually it came round to the topic of Chinese restaurants.

"Oh I'd send them all home". 'Dave' said as a matter of fact.
"Excuse me?" said 'Louise'
"Like I said, I'd send them all home"

The rest of the conversation involving 'Dave' was really rather nasty and unpleasant and therefore cannot be printed, but it was the way he spoke that was so unusual to me – he didn't raise his voice and there was no swearing or cursing in the style of the usual pub racist.

He was so sure of what he said and his voice and manner was that of, someone discussing the relative measures of the exchange rate currency fluctuation.

Playing devils advocate I said to him "What about my wife she's Chinese would you send her home".

He laughed, a bit embarrassed, and then said "Oh sorry, no offence mate".

'Louise' then said "but you've said it now and maybe offended someone,"

She continued with "if you get on this course and get an IT job you could end up working for a corporation where you will have to deal with people from India or Bangladesh"

"Yes but they'll be over there!" he said.

'Steve' and I took no further part in the conversation and I knew that beneath his quiet exterior 'Steve' was fuming. We had worked together for a while now and he had told me how multi cultural his previous workplace had been and how many colleagues had become personal friends.

Finally 'Louise' asked "Do you have a Chinese restaurant/take way near where you live?"

"Yeah, but they're alright" said 'Dave'.

Of all of us 'Dave' took the longest time to eat his meal. This was probably due to the fact that after every bite he stopped to make a point about some thing or another. He remarked that 'Debbie's mum found it incredibly annoying.

I think we could all sympathise with 'Debbie's mother and I imagined her clearing the dinner pots away in the same way that the restaurant waiters wiped up around us while he continued to prattle on.

As we got in the car the only thing 'Steve' and I could do was to laugh out loud, our thoughts on how 'Dave' and 'Debbie' could possible have got together made us feel it must have been some big joke.

I think I felt a little sympathy for 'Debbie' as my thoughts turned to consultancy open evenings/social events where you could bring your partner.

The evening was a real eye opener and I learned to be on my guard when expressing opinions with strangers or anyone really – you never know who might be listening and at what point they might come back to haunt you.

After an evening like that one I had certain thoughts about the sort of things I believed from what I had been hearing and seeing for myself over the years.

'Dave' had certainly opened my eyes as to how different people and groups have various ideas about immigrant workers coming to the UK, especially from the far and Middle East but also from Eastern Europe.

My view on this was formed by having stayed at several hotels.

Most of the staff in the hotels I encountered seemed to be eastern European students some of them didn't speak very good English. When I finally made it to the restaurant the service was almost laughable as we each tried to decipher what the other was asking for.

One particular night the evening meal took a long to arrive and I don't know if it was simply a custom thing, but all the tables around us were being laid for breakfast while we were still eating our evening meal.

Young people, in their late teens, early twenties or students, are in general the workforce in hotels, local pubs, restaurants and leisure centre's and many hotels are situated in the leafy suburbs of well to do villages.

The indigenous young people in these villages will (in my opinion), spend their weekends and evenings at Gymkhanas, Cricket matches and other high end and expensive social activities funded by 'daddy'.

The only other pool of staff being the nearest council estate might not be suitable, or even want to work for a minimum wage and training, to serve and clean in a hotel. For some it could be an inconvenience to have to take two buses to get to the hotel, or get in a car (which might look out of place in the car park). Would you as an employer, managing an expensive hotel or restaurant employ them?

No, I really do not think so.

The answer then is, to employ those that will. People from; Eastern Europe, Poland, Slovakia, or the Czech Republic will come to live and work in the Hotel under those conditions.

The drawback, for having foreign staff, for both the employer and the customer is that some of them don't speak very good English. On the other hand a good thing is that they can have a different approach, from their English counterparts, to dealing with problems.

One morning when coming down to check-out of the expensive, luxurious hotel (that I've spoken about), there was a long queue of people also waiting to check out and this queue stretched back into the bar area.

Everyone had things to attend to - consultants had to be on site, sales agents had calls to make and everyone had to be off and on their way.

Waiting in a queue as long as this was no fun and was potentially costing people money.

As we get closer to the front, shuffling our bags and suitcases along the floor, it became apparent that only one concierge, a young man from Eastern Europe with jet black hair greased straight back into a severe style and an immaculate shirt and tie, was on duty.

A Scottish man just in front of me was being very loud and aggressive. He had a thick Scottish accent - no one understood a word he was saying but I think it was absolutely crystal clear to everyone there, exactly what he meant.

Finally he got to the front of the queue and berated the concierge with his many complaints. The concierge in stilted English replied quietly.

"Sir, only Von Komputer is verking, shouting is futile"

This, I feel, shows the difference between the eastern Europeans and the British.

The concierge remained totally calm in the face if this aggressive behaviour (he probably did not understand a word the man was saying) and just pointed out the facts.

A British concierge would have raised their voice and replied with the excuse "It's not my fault, don't blame me, I'm doing my best" and ignored the facts, not allowing more discussion but turning it into an argumentative situation

Is this right?

Eventually I was fortunate enough to get a placement which meant that I was able to live at home, as the site was only an hours' drive away from home.
As a triathlete I find it very difficult to train when living on the road out of a suitcase. So being at home it was suddenly so much easier

Training for three sports is hard. There is the cycling gear and bike maintenance, running gear and perhaps the most difficult of all is finding time and places to fit in a swim.

But that's only the half of it.

I had been leaving the house at 6:30am, in order to get to the first swimming session of the day at the nearest pool for 7:30am. Having had a 45 minutes swim I would then leave to get to work for 8:30am

After work I would have a short run when I got home before I had my evening meal and then go cycling on Sundays.

Of course, you can't do any of these things, if you haven't eaten properly. (That is not a slur on my wife's cooking), I was just not taking in enough calories for what I was doing.

Maslow's hierarchy of needs applies to consultants and triathletes, just as much as it applies to anyone else.

So it was only to be expected that I had a particularly bad experience during a race and I decided that I was mentally and physically tired of being both a triathlete and a consultant, so I had a rest from training.

My time at home and my respite from driving long distances was short lived. Almost immediately after the end of my time locally I was called to another placement and I was living away from home again. I spent the next three months, eating hotel food, cooked breakfasts and putting on weight.

Generally I am not fat but I started to feel myself becoming sluggish so something had to change.

I bit the bullet and took my running gear down with me with the intention of going out running. I don't know if you, the reader, know anything about the psychology of amateur sport but what you need to understand is that when I say I needed to go for a run, it was the "need" of someone who really "needed" it and blow the consequences.

The hotel was on a dual carriage way. It was the middle of winter and running in the dark on a main road would not have been clever or safe.

So, one night when it was freezing cold, I put on my running gear got into the car. I had no idea where to go, so I just drove for about and ten minutes to a housing estate. It was the sort of place where everyone parks on their drive and not on the road, so I just abandoned the car and started running.

At that point I had no idea where I was - it was dark, freezing cold I was totally unfit and I thought to myself 'Why am I here why couldn't I have decided to do something else?'

I wasn't totally put off by that experience however and continued to find places more suitable to go for a run and after the running had become 'normal' I looked online to find a suitable swimming session nearby.

While online at one placement, I found a pool that was just off the ring road in the centre of a large UK city.

It was sign posted from the inner ring road near to the football ground but after a while the sign posts disappeared.

Pretty soon I was hopelessly lost and found myself driving around in a city centre estate where gangs of youths stood on street corners staring into my car when I stopped at traffic lights.

After driving around a few times and seeing the same youths again and again I was feeling a little perturbed and I found myself thinking 'why am I here?'
After an hour or so I got back to the hotel and the next day I bought a satellite navigation system.

Not allowing my couple of mishaps to hold me back, taking my running and swimming gear soon became a regular event (the bike never made it), but of course it meant taking yet another bag.
(Packhorse wanted!)

Certain family commitments meant my weeks on end travelling to work and living in hotels had to be curtailed, which brought some relief from the monotony of hotel living.

Up till that time my working week had been pretty much in the routine of:

Monday
Get up early, travel to site, work, then back to the hotel for the night (knackered)

Tuesday
Work, hotel

Wednesday
Work, go home Wednesday night, drive two hours, see kids, see wife, sleep in own bed.

Thursday
Get up early, travel to site two hours work, hotel.

Friday
Work, home Friday lunch-time if possible, Friday night (knackered)

Saturday
 Family

Sunday
Family

Monday repeat.

I was spending 8 hours a week (a full working day) in the driving seat which was too much for me.

I had a choice of alternatives to work with: work full time having a week off every six to seven weeks, or work part time, two to three days a week; Monday to Wednesday, Tuesday to Thursday.

So I chose to work part time. It still meant that I had to spend nights in a hotel and although it seems a pleasant idea to spend the night in an expensive hotel, it doesn't often relieve the problem of a good nights rest. In fact, even part time, Monday to Wednesday can just seem like one long day.

In fact on the days when I went home, I seemed to have an extra spring in my step. Throughout the day, I seemed a little happier with life and I never could get the words from the 1991 U2 track "Zoo Station" out of my head.

"It's alright, it's alright, I'm sleeping in my own bed tonight"

I had some very interesting times within the walls of; opulent, expensive and sometimes mediocre hotels, all expenses paid by the client, but as the 'help fund' started to dwindle, the agencies, found that clients were not as forthcoming with expenses money and in order to make some profit interims fees (certainly in my case) became 'pay inclusive'.

This is when your fee (which is what you agree to be paid) includes all your expenses. It is then in your own interest to find food and accommodation as cheaply as possible.

One particular event comes to mind.

I was working in a part of the country that had rolling fields, panoramic views and starry skies, but no hotels. The roads meandered across the countryside until I was sick of turning bend after bend then, lo and behold; I found a farmhouse B&B so I booked in.

When I first arrived at the farmhouse it looked OK (little did I know). I knocked on the door (the bell was broken) and it was answered by a dirty looking lady who showed me into the house. It was dark inside and the dingy looking walls were painted in a brown colour. The place smelt heavily of cigarette smoke and I thought about leaving but I didn't fancy the twisting roads in the dark.

I was led upstairs to my room which was very old fashioned, with a big wooden bed and old style wardrobe. The bathroom and toilet were of course downstairs. In my naivety, after having stayed in hotel rooms, I assumed all B&B's - although less classy - would still be en-suite.

The lady stood there with her hand out for the money.

So why did I say "thank you" instead of "no thank you"?

Well I had been up before 06.00 driven 2 hours on the motorway and was starting a new job with all the mental resolve that entails. Having only had a sandwich for lunch I had missed out on an evening meal. I was hungry and tired.

Then to top it all, I had naively assumed that all B&B's took credit cards. I had no cash on me so I had to drive back along the narrow roads anyway and into the nearest town find the cash point and draw some money out, to pay the lady!

The next morning I got out of there as quickly as possible and began looking for somewhere – anywhere- else to stay. I was directed to another Farmhouse B&B that had been posted on the council's website by one of the staff at the site I was attending.

This farmhouse was so very different from the last one I had stayed in. It was clean, fresh looking and airy, and from this haven I was able to explore the area and its endless country lanes especially as the weather was improving and summer was on its way.

I must say that exploring country lanes on a summers evening is one of the best parts of being a runner.

One evening I set off in bright warm sunshine, got caught in a summer rainstorm then came back in warm bright sunshine – my legs were tingling I was soaking wet, then I looked into the sky and I saw a rainbow.

I remember thinking that there was nowhere else I would have rather been at that time.

There I was, over seventy miles away from home and family, soaking wet, staying in a strange place and feeling a little bit guilty because I loved it.

The owners of the farmhouse B&B were extremely friendly and helpful. It turned out that I was in fact their first ever customer and they couldn't do enough for me. It was a great place to talk about other things apart from work. and not only did I have a freshly cooked breakfast, sometimes I was invited to join them for their evening meal, which meant that on some days the only time I actually had to fend for myself was lunchtime.

The warm weather encouraged me to go out at lunchtimes looking for suitable eating places and from then on I continued to leave the office not only to try the local fare but because I have always enjoyed the fresh air and to be alone to read a magazine/paper or look at the area around but more importantly it meant that I did not have to be in the office.

If you are at your desk people will continue to treat you as if you are working.

You will be disturbed by someone with the line "I know you are on your lunch…but can I just ask you about…."

My solution and one that I would encourage all managers to do was to get a newspaper.

I always used the "Daily Telegraph" (It shows a bit more intelligence – than the "Sun" or the "Mirror" although the "Guardian" is quite trendy for people with soft shoes, beards and woolly cardigans), apologies for the prejudice – but hey – this is my book.

Anyway, I used the paper as a psychological 'Do Not Disturb' sign whenever I was in the office or the sandwich bar.

What did I do when alone at evening mealtimes?

Evening meals sat by your self, in a hotel or restaurant night after night can be a bit tricky and can make you look a bit of a 'saddo'.

So depending on where I was staying I chose from the following.

Hotel Restaurant: "All inclusive" – (cost of the meal was included in my daily fee).

It was always a bit awkward, sitting at a fully set formal table because that made it difficult to spread out the newspaper.
Reading a book was a little better but I never felt as relaxed as I did with a newspaper.
A book gives the message 'I am alone' a newspaper is more - I am 'chilling out'.

Less formal restaurants – Attached to a pub or bar. Same rules applied but it was much easier to spread out my paper. Local pubs were often busy with large groups and err... locals. When I was on my own it felt pretty lonely and I found it best to arrive early while the place was still relatively quiet, then slip out again even though it meant going back to the four walls of the hotel room.

Farmhouse/ B&B – with no restaurant or eating on site I had to drive to find an eating place.
A take away, McDonalds/KFC at the nearest town occasionally sufficed but I did not forget my newspaper.
Choose wisely; was the motto of the moment.

Nothing on site – no suitable pub/restaurant near the B&B was the hardest choice of all. I found it best to go with a cooked breakfast followed with sandwich/pasties for lunch and was thus able to survive the evening by 'eating' the dreaded pot noodle.

Room Service – this was often quicker than the restaurant or bar in a hotel.

The first time I had room service was a novelty for a country yokel like me.
I had worked out that it arrived faster than food ordered at the bar.
(This may be because a pretty waitress has to come over to soft soap you to smooth over any delays while you sit and wait in the restaurant).

The first time my room service arrived, it was a steaming hot plate of whatever it was I had ordered and a cold pint of lager, I also had football on the TV on. Sitting there I was almost childlike in my feelings of excitement.

If I wasn't alone then of course everything was so much easier. The newspaper stayed in my room unless I really disliked the colleague I was working with, or the colleague was in another hotel, but that was a rare occasion, Most of the time I found that I would be dining with my friends

Final thoughts

During my time as an interim I was able to meet so many more interesting people than I could ever have done if I had stayed in my first (safe) job.

I have my prejudices and my 'bugbears' about people, places and the ways that they do things, which I know could be done so much better, but I have also been surprised by many of them and in some cases shocked out of my prejudices so I include this last incident as a moral tale...

I was to receive a visit from a representative of a large PLC operating in the public sector. The Director of the place I was working at requested that I see her to find out "what was going on". (In reality, what was she trying to sell).

This lady was expected at 11:00 am It was mid winter and cold but clear. She rang to say that she would be late – her car windscreen washer bottle was leaking and she had to go to a motorway service station to get it sorted out, and it would be an hour before the AA got to the station (to do a two minute job)..

When she finally arrived she requested that I fill the bottle up. So I trooped out in to the freezing cold with a bottle of water thinking "This isn't in my job description" and then searched around to find out where to pour the water into the washer bottle of a mini cooper.

Before the start of the meeting she apologized again because she had broken her glasses and would have to wear her prescription sunglasses, for the duration of the meeting.

After that there was a third apology to explain that she did not have a pen, paper or diary (these, had been left at the motorway service station) so could she please borrow some and could she use the phone and did I have her HQ's main switchboard number handy because her mobile battery was flat and she needed to report that she was running late.

At this point I hope I can be forgiven for thinking that this person was at best slightly comical and at worst completely incompetent.

However, as soon as the meeting started her attitude changed from 'little girl lost' into some sort of secret service interrogator. Who did I know? What did I think? How much did this cost? Why did I get a discount?

Being pumped for information for an hour or so is not very pleasant and it was made even worse because I had not been expecting it.

The old adage 'Don't judge a book by its cover' was very relevant. I was only glad that I hadn't voiced my opinion of the lady before I had actually met her as 'Dave' had done with us at our restaurant dinner.

Collection of thoughts on management

Professional managing skills

You might have read the first few chapters of this book, or you might just have skipped to this part in your anticipation of learning something useful, but however you have got to this point this is not meant to be a management text book, its just a collection of my thoughts on things I have learnt while doing interim consultancy and management and things I have placed in my management toolbox, should I need them in the future.

Some of them apply to any situation, but some are specific to things that I have done and you may find them interesting even if you never need to use them.

I'll start with some terms which may need defining.

A manager; is the person in charge of a complete workgroup. In the case of housing benefit this person is called the 'Benefits Manager (surprise, surprise)
His/her immediate underlings will be a 'team leader' or 'assistant manager'.

A consultant: is someone who is brought in to diagnose a problem or to provide a suggestion for a course of action. Very much like a hospital consultant. Kept at arms length; they come in and dispense words of wisdom, (usually with a PowerPoint presentation), then leave.

An Interim Manager is someone brought in to cover for the manager when he/she is unable to do their current job. This is slightly different to a consultant because an Interim Manager can become part of the fabric of the office. They are much more likely to get to know the staff.

The interim managers 'job' can be split into two sub-categories:

The first is 'minding the shop' - The interim is brought in to maintain the status quo –everything is allowed to carry on ticking along nicely, no real problems just awaiting the return of the manager.

The second is 'critical friend' – which includes diagnosing problems then providing the solutions (and running the office if there is any time left).

The difference between a consultant and interim manager/consultant can sometimes be very subtle.

I can often tell, when I go to events and presentations that the speaker has been a consultant as their presentations will often include giveaway words like; vision, strategy and inspiration. These are words that the average person just doesn't use.

A manager/interim manager on the other hand has to deliver the solutions to the many visions, strategies and inspirations that have been focused on, and if you don't deliver you're out.

The art of Management

A Good Director

I expect a director to direct activity. This might sound obvious but most Directors I have met either want to be; the chief clown in the style of TV's - David Brent (the creation of Ricky Gervais) or the invisible man/woman because you never see them from one week to the next.

In my view a good director should be like a guide in the Himalayan mountains.

"OK we are going up that hill it's steep so I'll go first and be back to pick up any one who is struggling. Let's go everybody."

A good director should understand the output required from their service and the risks and problems of achieving this. They do not have to do it themselves but should get in place people that can.

A good manager should possess the planning insights of the director and lead with the common touch of a supervisor.
Unfortunately in most places I've worked, when someone becomes a manager they think they just need to do their existing job but better.

Delegation v Organisation

One common definition of management is" getting things done through other people"

Many people confuse delegation with organisation so here is a simple guide:

Organisation: - is organising people and resources to get things done. On the simplest level it could be a team leader organising lunch breaks so that the office is covered over the break.
Organising lunch breaks isn't a good use of management time and so the key is to delegate some management functions.

Delegation: - means that a manager can ask a subordinate staff member to do part of the managers' job without extra pay or necessarily wider recognition.

For example
Barack Obama talks about improving health care in America, but I doubt he will do much work in a hospital in any of the States during his term in

office; he just has to make sure that the work gets done.

So in the Barack Obama example; he will remain responsible (to the American people) but he has delegated the task of improving health care to people lower down in his organisational team.

Delegating successfully means several things:

Firstly you must trust the person you are delegating to do the task. This is not only to trust them not to foul up the task but to keep you posted as to its progress.

Secondly, there are likely to be issues of skill level and training. No one would expect an untrained person to carry out a skilled or specialist tasks (safety considerations etc.)

Thirdly, there is the art of selecting the right person. Not everyone is able or willing to do more than what is on their job description. Quite often a 'jobs worth' mentality can prevent some people from even entertaining the idea!

The good news is that if you are able to delegate successfully and find someone to trust, it will feel like you have grown a spare pair of hands. Things get done without you necessarily asking and the trusted staff members point of view, learning new skills and improving is a good way to prepare for a promotion or career move.

I would always look to 'bend' the rules for someone who had shown initiative and done more than they needed to (after all that's what they were asking of me).

So either way, learning to delegate (or at least knowing the difference between delegation and organisation) is an essential management skill to learn.

3. A good team leader
The front line supervisor or team leader should be someone who can hold down six or eight desks worth of holiday requests, return to work/sickness interviews and allocate work that is not a management function, to prevent the manager getting drawn into discussions about who will leave at 4:00pm and other trivial matters.

4. Workers
The workers must work within the skill levels they have. They shouldn't act like directors, supervisors or managers but should be treated with respect by the manager, even when airing their opinions.

So in a nutshell these four levels should do their part and only their part or the structure will fall down…

How management can irritate people without really trying

Here are two stories which illustrate how management can alienate and even annoy staff without even knowing they are doing it.

I once worked in a large rectangular open plan office with 2 doors - one at each end of one of the "long sides".

It was the last working day before Christmas Eve and general merriment abounded which I was quite happy to allow.

All gaiety and laughter instantly stopped as the Director (who had never been seen out of his enclave before) decided it was his 'meet the troops' time, he opened the door (it went VERY quiet) and he gave his, "Good wishes to you and your families" speech and left again – quiet hushed conversation had just re-started when we heard it all go quiet in the office next door. We knew he had entered and repeated the same speech as before.

He went away with that "I think I know that place and those people but I am not sure" confused look on his face.
The staff thought he was a buffoon and did not have much respect for him.

The second story concerns rubbish

In the last 5-10 years the way in which councils deal with rubbish & refuse collection has been completely turned on it's head. As a child, I can remember when bin men used to come down our drive to collect the bin, lift it onto their shoulders and carrying it up the driveway to the waiting lorry.

Wheelie bins started to change all that and more recently, green bins, brown bins, blue boxes, bags etc has pushed a lot of responsibility back to the customer. (Which I generally agree with).

I was working in a council which was trying very hard to counter the publicity the local press was dishing out about rubbish collection (This was a quiet part of the country and slow ticket sales at the annual Christmas panto were big news). I was introduced to the Public Relations officer who told me how irritated he had been with the director and the reason for it.

The publicity officer had suggested (and it was agreed by management) that all concerned were to avoid the "F" (fortnightly collections) word at all costs.

The media had been stirring the pot, trying to paint a picture of rubbish piling up for weeks on end and council workers having a week off. The word "fortnightly" emphasised this.

The counter attack was the key line "alternate weeks" – this gives the impression of working in a set timetable not in an unspecified time scale.

The Public Relations Officer, told me that he had worked really hard getting the 'alternate week's' message over.

Staff had all had briefings – customers using the "F" word should be politely but firmly corrected to using 'alternate weeks.'

He was even thinking of running an internal campaign featuring "Dad's army" type characters and the "Don't use the F- word" strap line.

Then he went away on holiday and when he returned, the local paper had emailed him asking for details of the 'fortnightly' collection.

"Who said fortnightly?" he rang to ask them.

"Oh it was your Mr "Directors name" – you were on holiday"

And there it was, undone in a flash – all that hard work and ironically – by the supposed top man.

I know this story is second hand but it does illustrate the point of everyone being on message and that message coming from the top down. Everyone should share the message so intently, "discipline" and motivation is not needed, and irritating mistakes are banished.

Legitimacy and trust

Legitimacy is something that is very important for an interim. You are a complete stranger to the in-house staff and you will have to show them that you are not just some bozo who has turned up in a suit to tell them what to do.

Quite often internal people can be negative and less than co-operative, even to the point of being "hostile" to some one new. This has not happened to me personally, but I have spoken to colleagues who have sat at their desks with a 'tin hat' on to protect themselves from all the 'flack'.

One of my first assignments was within a small Local Authority. It was so small that you could regularly see the chief executive eating his dinner in the canteen, or just bobbing around the open-plan offices.

I made it my business to make him aware of what it was I was doing and what I'd seen. After all a good consultant should not shirk, from telling bad news to his client (it shows off analytical skills if nothing else).

He invited me in for a progress chat and from what I'd seen, I warned him of an 'impending disaster'.

He leaned forward and said

"Jonathan you have my personal authority to do whatever you feel to avoid any disruption of services. If you need staff training, software, whatever, just let Tracy (his secretary), know and it's yours."

I didn't realize it at the time but this gave me great power, especially if ever anyone had raised a doubt or a query about a project I'd started.

My approach to this gaining of power can be summed up in two words I once heard at a seminar and these are "authoritative" and "assumptive".

Imagine taking a relative to A&E with what you suspect is a badly broken arm. S/he is in a lot of pain and you go in to see the consultant who starts by saying

"If it's OK with you, I am just going to think about what I'm going to do about this, have a look online and read a book or two and then maybe we could try…?"

You would not be very impressed.

But to hear

"This is the problem, your arm is broken and what we are going to do this…."

Is much more reassuring don't you think?

The 'do you mind if I…' approach would not have worked well for the clients who hired me. Some had problems in very dysfunctional services and wanted them fixed

I had to show my authority – not be stamping about and throwing my weight around - that is a good way to annoy people and usually makes it almost impossible to build trust.

One thing I am lucky about is having a very distinctive Sheffield accent.

OK it's not distinctive in Sheffield, but go 100 miles down the motorway and people think you have come from another planet.

For those of you who don't know the Sheffield/South Yorkshire accent has a dropped 'T' and 'H" sound.

As one young lady pointed out –"You talk funny, you miss words out".

For example "put t'kettle on" or "going t'supermarket"

The t in t'kettle is not pronounced hard but soft the two words "put kettle" are rolled together as one. However, the t in t'supermarket IS pronounced. (Don't ask me why)

Of course many people found this interesting and even charming. Attempts by non Sheffielders at replicating it frequently fail.

The Sheffield accent is generally accepted as quite a friendly one (I once read that the South Yorkshire area is favoured by big corporations looking to site call centres) and 'hamming it up', I could make myself noticed and stand out without being loud and noisy.

So once they had got used to the accent and I knew that they understood what I was saying, I decided on an approach which showed, that I could see what the problem was and then assume, without having to check with management, that I had enough authority to carry out the solution in the hope that nobody would think I was being a 'know all'?

It allowed me to get along with people and at the same time be in charge. I called it the 'only just smarter than them' approach

Because most information, especially in local government, is sent around offices electronically, it is possible that by knowing and using the functionality of the software you can get that 'I know something you don't know I know' feeling and also be able to tell when the wool is being pulled over your eyes.

Email has become a corporate insurance policy. Messages can be sent to multiple people and cc – ing it to (copying it) your boss lets them know (in a more subtle way than going into their office in front of everyone) what's going on.

Without being underhand or devious about it, it is possible to set your email software to 'spy' on internal people who receive your messages and from that work out:

How long it took them to open it? - You might be surprised by how many people open just seconds after having just received mail.
Whether they deleted it?
How long it took them to read it?

Knowing something and then finding out who knew what and when, allows you to be 'only just smarter than them'

Did you know that in 'Word' (or any other Microsoft application) you can view details on the age and history of a document - when it was created and how many times it has been saved?

Not just in software - there are certainly other methods of being 'only just smarter than them' which include:

Using confident body language – especially on your first day
Watching their body language and acting accordingly to it.
Using certain types of questions - asking smart and/or complicated questions will either 'phase' staff or 'scare' them (most staff will try to give you the answer they think you want, which isn't always

helpful) and you will tend to get simple 'yes' or 'no' answers.

Simple questions like: "Why do you do that like that?", "Who told you to do it?" "What is that for?" were more likely to get the answers and information I wanted, because staff would generally give an explanation with their answers (as long as I reassured them they weren't in trouble).

I don't mind admitting now that I was very lucky that so early on in my career as an interim this chief executive had given me the authority and therefore the legitimacy to be in charge.

With that I gained the confidence to be able to face the staff with assurance and the staff in turn, assumed that I was someone who knew what he was doing.

With this feeling of legitimacy I entered offices without being afraid that I was going to be harangued by the staff and was soon talking to them and finding out about their positions in the authority/business. It was possible then to find out within the first few days/hours which of the in-house people I could trust.

That's not trust in the conventional sense, but rather trusting someone to carry out tasks, objectives and functions.

To have a desk where?

This is a debate I have had with several colleagues in several placements.

The problem is;
Do you go for your own desk in the main office?
Or do you have your own personal / shared office.

A desk in the main office means that you are much more likely to pick up on the general vibes of the place much more quickly. People are often very indiscrete when gossiping about office matters and you can often overhear some very useful titbits.

The downside to this is you can get involved with trivialities that really have nothing to do with you.

Your own personal or shared office has its advantages in that you aren't disturbed by the prattle of others and can get on with the work with relatively few interruptions.
The downside is that you may be seen by the staff as the 'Prat in the office' who will hide in there, if the proverbial hits the fan.

Of course you will be suspected of plotting and planning if the door is shut.

The solution to the problem is perhaps to have a 'hot desk' – to move around the different workstations every few weeks. This means you get a good feel of the overall area quite quickly – you can also move in and out of your office. When people have seen you they might start to trust you.

Having said all that, I am not at my desk very often.

One of the required texts on my degree course was written by the management 'guru' Tom Peters. His concept was MBWA – Management by Walking About

I follow this idea and prefer to 'tour the floor' and always find out what is happening first hand. (Rudolph Giuliani, Mayor of New York at the time of the 9/11 attacks also used this concept successfully)

If I ever did get my own office, I soon learned to remove any nearby chairs to discourage people from sitting down for a chat.

Working out who is who

When you enter any office, it will be pretty easy to work out the hierarchy by looking at who sits where, who has a tidy desk or a messy one. It may be that the most important person in the office sits right in the middle of it.

This person is usually the one everyone seems to turn to or rely upon. Observing what happens when visitors arrive and who they gravitate towards for help, is also an effective way to find this person. Most offices have one.

Let's say the individual concerned is a team leader called Doris:

When you ask Doris why something happens in a certain way, she will give you an extremely long explanation starting with minor events from 5-10 years ago.

Her desk will be a complete shambles and her phone will ring constantly.

Doris will be the one to sort out all manner of the trivial items that really do not need to concern her and if she is going on holiday (which is rare), everyone gets worried in advance and the general topic of conversation is "How will we cope without Doris"

Doris is likely to think that everyone else is a complete fool and/or unable to carry out her job in any way as well as she does. 'Things can't run without her'

Quite often Doris may be off sick with minor illnesses (colds, sore throat, upset stomach, water infections, which are in fact all signs of stress) or alternatively she is NEVER off sick.

My approach would always be to wait until the end of a working day to chat informally to this sort of person, as most of the time they would be the only one left in the office still working. For them to be able to trust me was very important.

Talking to other staff, throughout the day helped me to be aware of the office atmosphere.

Some offices at different placements had an undercurrent of anger and frustration at the removal of the manager I was replacing, old loyalties die hard, while at others they felt as though the cavalry had arrived

Ultimately these findings would help me work out who I might be able to trust to do things apart from 'Doris'. Then, having found out who I could trust it was a case of finding out if the staff would trust me.

To a great extent a key consultancy skill is establishing the trust of the internal workforce; be they in-house staff, team leader, whatever. Once you have got that, you will get a constant stream of visitors to your desk.

One particular technique of mine to gain trust was to do something on the first few days that would be to try to relieve them of a problem.

I was asked "Could you speak to "Mr. Angry" over the phone. He was a regular caller and nobody like talking to him so I spoke to him found out what his real problem was, and then got it sorted out with the help of other members of staff.

At other times and in other places I would take some work which might have been troubling them for a long time or tried to solve a problem they had,

I knew that even if I failed, as long as it didn't make the problem any worse they knew I was trying to do it for them.

I even delivered some training to put myself in the chair as a 'subject matter' expert, anything that would give them something which showed they were in a safe pair of hands.

Respect and credibility

If you are seen to be willing to put yourself about a bit for them, staff will start to accept you. Every site has customers that staff would prefer not to deal with and this is very understandable as the general public seems to be growing increasingly rude, aggressive and arrogant.

To earn their respect as well as their trust I always tried to front up to these 'bullish' sorts of individuals.

I remember that on one occasion an elderly gent was particularly aggressive with bad language and fierce expression, to a young lady on staff and I stepped in and took over the situation.

The gentleman then threatened me by suggesting that he would go to the chief executive and report how 'unhelpful' I had been.

At the time I thought to myself 'Do I really care whether he reports me or not. After all I can only get the sack' and. I'm sure the chief executive will see through an elderly 'gentleman' being rude and aggressive" (unless of course he happened to be a friend and neighbour of the Chief Exec').

Dealing with these people in front of the staff tended to put a notch or two on the respect board.

However respect and credibility can be lost far more quickly and easily than it can be won and my managing tip here is: - Do not disrespect or bad mouth the person you have been brought in to replace, at any point, even if some of the staff do.

You may have learnt, from your Director or in a previous briefing how incompetent or inefficient the person you replace may have been, but internal staff members can have friends and loyalties in other departments. If colleagues have worked together for a long time they can develop a strong relationship.

For example Manager A (the person you are covering for) and Manager B in another section could have worked together for a long time.

Manager B sees Manager A's problems as problems with the organisation – if you come along and say "No manager A was, this that and the other…." It won't go down very well with some and will lose you credibility.

My second management tip is: to move cautiously when taking control of, what is for you, a new group of staff. Yes, you may be tempted to make sweeping changes quickly but don't move too fast.

One particular office had 2 'mature' men working in it. They were probably in their late 40's early 50's but that was where the similarity between them ended.

The first had been made redundant from a local factory. He had been the office clerk and had left with a large redundancy payment. He had spent it all and a lot more besides and was now in financial difficulty and needed the job he was doing. He spent most of his time moaning about football.

The second had been a local bank manager. His redundancy was a large pension with 'perks'. He went abroad at every opportunity and wandered around the office as though he had no cares in the world. The job was a 'hobby' for him, with a bit of pin money for golf as well as looking for someone to talk to.

Looking at them at the outset, it seemed that they would have been a good pair to do a task or a project together, fortunately I didn't just jump in and make the that mistake as it turned out that neither man could stand the sight of the other.
I could so easily have slipped up and lost any credibility for making changes within the office.

I have spoken a lot about gaining the respect and looking credible in the eyes of the staff and that is all very well, but it is also important that, when given the go ahead to do something from the Director or client that you maintain their respect too. When it comes down to it they are the ones who will give you the boot if you make a mess of it.

The following story can show how you can lose some credibility by the choices you make but then regain your status by taking decisive action.

At one placement, I was working with a colleague; we inherited a severe backlog of work without enough in-house staff to get through it.

So, in our role as consultants my colleague and I put a package of figures together, gave it to the assistant director, our 'boss', and told him that if he wanted this backlog clearing it would take 3 months and cost £30,000

He gave us the go ahead and we recruited 3 members of staff and a team leader from a recruitment agency.

They were placed in a separated area of the building and the work was piped up to them via the document management system.

It soon became obvious that the team was not functioning correctly.

We had inkling that they were using the internet extensively. Not being stupid, I would regularly go up to see them on a "wellbeing visit" and a simple tactic of opening the door quickly and bursting in on them meant they would panic move to click their open "football results window" to a more work related one.

One of them was in fact the third highest user of the internet in the whole of the organisation for one particular week.

This was our mistake - here we were, two very capable interim consultants and we had made a big mess of recruiting the right staff

This was a situation that couldn't continue. We were responsible for bringing the contractors in. We knew that the management was still a bit suspicious of consultants, and we were concerned that this would show us in a bad light.

So on December 23rd we took the decision to terminate the employment of three of the contract team at an hours notice due to gross misconduct and misuse of the internet. My colleague went to see the assistant director and when he returned, I asked what he had said, the director had apparently been "quite pleased" to have seen some action being taken by management.

We had made a mistake but our credibility held due to the actions we had taken. We hadn't tried to hide it, but confronted it straight on.
The consultancy cycle
Legitimacy, respect and trust do in fact take time to build and I am not suggesting that within a week or

two you will have them all, but the foundations for earning them does however begin on day one.

In almost every placement, in the first few days, if not the first day, I would receive; visits, phone calls and emails from staff about a whole host of matters some important some trivial.
With all this information coming in I found that it was best, initially, to never take anyone's word for anything.

On being sworn in President Jimmy Carter was being shown around the Whitehouse on his first day. He was given the suitcase which contained the buttons to press in case of nuclear attack.
The conversation is said to go something like this:

"OK Mr. President sir, any problems, day or night, press this button and a helicopter will be on the landing pad within 15 minutes".
"Fifteen minutes?" replied President Carter.
"Yes sir, fifteen minutes day or night".
"Do it now!" he said

Fifteen minutes passed with no helicopter, then thirty and finally, so the story goes, it was nearly forty minutes before the helicopter was available.

A fundamental weakness (sometimes called an "urban myth") was exposed because President Carter had challenged, what he had been told so confidently by, his staff.

So in the first few days and weeks, I would check up on minutes of meetings, official publications, the Internet, the intranet, shared files and drives.

People will always believe that what they are doing is the most important bit for you to look at but there will be so much more.

I got demographic information about the area and where and who the customers are and only then could I formulate a plan in my head as to what is important and what is not.

What I learnt from these things and what you think you are going to do about them is dangerous to share with staff, as they will take everything literally and want to run with it; the truth is that a lot of what I considered ended up on the floor discarded and for this reason you should be very careful sending out emails and guarded in what you say.

There were many times when I found yourself crashing into inefficient procedures and processes which people have been working with for a long time.

The easiest way to describe this is; when you visit someone's home and sees a clock not telling the right time or a wonky picture, the owner of the house has got used to these things and works around them. You as a visitor can't help but put the clock right.

You need to imagine those trivial things multiplied in a busy service. People are required to work around procedures and processes that are just a little bit wonky, but which could leave them dissatisfied, upset, stressed, and angered without realizing the problem.

Communication & language

As a manager I like to encourage a sense of openness and communication between the staff and myself.

I feel that the last thing the staff would want to see is some bloke, they've never seen before, coming in and changing things without telling them why.

Unfortunately there are people who tend to try to take advantage of this.
People who would come to me and say something along the lines of 'why don't we just' and 'it would be good if we could do this and that' and 'every time we try the other something goes wrong but you can sort that out'.

At first I appreciated any positive suggestions from staff but then I realized that if I said "yes" to every one it would create a whole pile of extra work for myself.

People are great at sitting on the sidelines pointing out what is to be done and how it should be done but they are not so good at getting it done themselves.

I learned there were several categories of people and often when they say "we could do this" they really mean you could.

What I learned was that when somebody said 'it would be great if we could do this or that'. My answer to them would be "OK you have my approval to go ahead, take - 30 minutes, a couple of days or whatever to get some ideas together, there's no money in the budget but if you could write a report by the end of next week on how its going that would be great".

Most of the time the idea would mysteriously go away and very rarely did I get the said report so they obviously didn't feel that strongly about it.

Pretty soon they stopped suggesting things and returned to what they were supposed to be doing.

However, I would say that when I did get feedback, some of it was very good.

It wasn't always, in the form it was given to me, something I could give straight to the director, but these people definitely earned some brownie points in my eyes, especially as their input wasn't a moan – which we are all good at – but an objective account of their ideas written down.

Using language
We all know that language is important and you will probably know all about the use of positive and negative words in getting your point over.

When we speak we usually work out, from the feedback of the other person whether or not we have made ourselves clear. We do this is by looking for facial expressions, and listening for the ummms and ahhhs in the expected places.
If we have not made ourselves clear we can immediately check and rephrase...

In "The People Whisperer" by Perry Wood, he states that most people just throw their words out in any old order and then rearrange them so they make sense to the listener.

Why do most people say that they hate hearing themselves on tape or on video?
It's because they get feedback on themselves - and quite often it's not pleasant.
Seeing ourselves as others do can be quite painful and maybe this is a factor in the rapid growth of management by email - where managers just send out emails with multiple word documents attached.

It's safer because there is no immediate feedback from the recipient.

What does this mean for the manager?

When was the last time you listened to what you are saying or thought for a second about the impact of your words on the listener/s?

Here is an example...
One manager I was working with repeatedly used the word "they" when referring to another department.

The use of the word "they" de-personalised the other department and undid all the other good work, done by that manager, to build bridges and mend fences between the different teams because, for his staff, it became "them" and "us".

When staff use the word "they" to customers when referring to another department, it reduces the member of staff or the team to be something or body to be got through. The guardian of "them" if you like.

This is multiplied if there is a problem or dispute. If I was a customer and someone continuously used the word "they" to me, I would say "OK – just go and get them…"

When I (politely) pointed this out - the manager concerned was horrified and vowed never to do it again...

Hypnotic words

Sales & Marketing professionals use a phrase called "hypnotic words". These are words which the author or speaker uses to "hypnotise" (not literally) the reader or listener into doing or thinking something.

Unfortunately, we all use hypnotic words without always realising. Here is an example.

You go to the dentist and are sat in the chair. The dentist says "this won't hurt"

You do one of several things

1. Wait for it to start hurting
2. Wonder if the dentist has the same pain threshold as yourself
3. Wish you were somewhere else.

Either way, when the dentist says "this will not hurt, the first thing you think of is … hurt…"

That's because the dentist has "hypnotised" you

Of course we can be hypnotised both ways, positive and negative (that's called guerrilla words…)

Examples

A contact centre officer receives a call from an irate customer. This is what the officer says.

"So I can help you solve this problem fast, please give me your reference number"

3 hypnotic words, help, solve problem, fast

As managers, if we are conscious of the language we use, we can "hypnotise" people or not. (Ethically of course)

"Please do not hesitate to contact me" (guess the hypnotic word…)

Dextifing

It is precisely because businesses (Local government in particular) do not encourage people to go out on a line or to take risks. That when people say something in a team meeting or whatever they will feel the need to 'dextify' it.

What is 'dextify'? I hear you say.

I think 'dextify' came from an old customer services course I went on a long time ago.

It is made up from combining the three words- defend, explain and justify.
When people 'dextify', their intentions are totally positive but it almost always comes over as negative.

Here is an example

You receive a letter of complaint from a customer about waiting times in the customer service area.

A good holding response would be:

Dear customer
Re: delays in the customer service area

Thank you for your letter regarding the above. I am sorry you experienced delays in the customer service area. As you know all our service staff are highly trained to make sure all problems are dealt with thoroughly. I have passed your letter on to the customer services manager to deal with the issues you raised personally. He will be replying by the end of the week.

Yours Sincerely

Manager

As a holding letter, reply, it does' just enough' to be satisfactory without accepting blame.

It reassures the recipient that the author is sorry for the delays they will receive a personal reply from the Customer Services Manager (and a timescale for this to happen).

Imagine if you will, how the whole meaning of the letter would be altered if the following paragraph were added to the bottom;

"I have passed your letter on to the customer services manager who informs me that delays and waiting times have actually decreased over the last 12 months (graph enclosed) and compare very well with neighbouring authorities (graph also enclosed). He also informed me that staff training courses have an unavoidable side effect of causing customer delays"

Do you see what happened?

The whole tone of the letter changed, by trying to defend, explain and justify the delay. If anything it will have succeeded in winding the customer up several more notches.

1. Graphs and charts don't mean anything to the customer and they are not interested about the last 12 months, they may have only just moved into the area.
2. Nobody cares about what the neighbouring authorities do.
3. Silly old customer – they thought staff training was meant to prevent delays not cause them.

The bottom line is, say what you have to say, don't try to 'dextify' too much and you will appear stronger and much more assured.
Using technologies and software.

Having worked in my own home-based business for some time now I have noticed that there is a big difference in the IT support I get now and the support I was getting as a consultant/interim.

In your home office you don't have PC support to call on. If you contracted some of this out you could have some support, but on the whole, with forgotten passwords, jammed monitors, stuck printers and viruses you pretty much have to paddle your own canoe

I find this very frustrating and even as I write this sentence I sit waiting for an unresponsive programme to respond.

In an office/company business when your PC, Software, or printer doesn't work you just ring someone, or get someone else to ring, the IT helpdesk. In a large business that's quite easy because there are loads of spotty faced kids who will generally do things for you as long as you are polite, friendly and helpful and this was the case in almost every place that I worked.

However, in one place the IT support was contracted out to a large PLC and to log a call for something as basic as a jammed printer you had to (unbelievably) ring a call centre in Bangladesh who would ring back and assign the job to an appropriate worker and then a man would come from the office next door, once he'd had his work assigned, to sort it out

If you are you thinking about a career as an independent consultant, you will need to consider just how much you know about computers and IT.

Attitudes to IT
I believe that there are two IT generations in 2009
First there is my generation, those who choose to use IT and computers.

I include myself in this. I have an O level in Computer Studies and unless I had chosen otherwise, my IT knowledge would have died with the BBC Micro from 25 years ago.

We tend to learn as we go along; after all the technology is not hard (My father of 75+ years uses word processing and shops online quite often). Our generation will do only as much as we need to with various software. Getting out of our comfort zones is a big step for us.

Then there is the next generation who don't choose to use technology, it is thrust upon them. People who reached their mid teens in the early part of this century when broadband became just another utility, are born into a world of; pixels, RSS feeds, downloads and USB memory sticks and they just get on with it.

Most of the places I have been too have had the IT thrust upon them by the needs of the service but these people really belong in the generation of 'choose to use' and this can be a real problem when they are given some software and minimal training and expected to "get on with it".

From a systems design view it can become a massive problem.

Here's a simple illustration
'Pauline' has to log onto her PC every day. She types in her password >password< because it's easy to remember (other passwords might include simple words like: Beckham, Arsenal, etc. Pauline is never happy with passwords; she remembers when you could leave your front door unlocked at night…)

Two unknown windows open up automatically and she has to close them before logging on.

"What are they for? I ask.

"I don't know. Sometimes three windows open and then I have to restart the computer" is her answer.

"Why is that?"

"I don't know"

"Have you tried to fix it?"

"Well I rang Gary in IT and he just laughed at me"

"So he didn't know either?"

Pauline laughs "No I suppose not"

If you were to think about it, the number of closing down clicks and the time it takes to re-boot and all the restarts could add up to,10 or more, minutes of non-productive time each week.

If Pauline worked for 41 weeks per year the result adds up to almost 8 hours of no work.

It is plausible that "Gary" would not take 8 hours to fix the problem and uneconomic to imagine that Pauline should sit and stare at her computer for one day a year.

NOTE – of course it's not just ten minutes each week; if the boot-up error happens on Thursdays Pauline has a conversation with her friend Carol about last nights TV, which must be finished before she returns to the computer to login.

And because Carol is not confident enough (or just not allowed) to tinker with the settings of her PC, a small road block has been created.
I have pointed out to managers in some places that:
- sometimes managing the 'trivialities' in the workplace can have a dramatic effect on output. Here is another example.

The Group Printer

The printer (like the photocopier) may not be seen so much as an IT tool because they have been around for so long and are generally easy to use but they can cause as many problems for IT working as any virus.

I have never been to a workplace where the area around the printer is clean and tidy. It is usually an area of utter devastation.

Most people don't realize that, like computers themselves, modern printers and software have evolved and many of them now have clever functions which can print onto headed paper from one tray, print onto plain paper from another or print the word "DRAFT' or "CONFIDENTIAL" onto the document.
In this day and age they can even queue letters, to print at the end of the day or during a quiet lunchtime.

Just as in the generation analogy for working with computers, working with printers is the same.

Here's a simple illustration to show the how easily "roadblocks" can be formed by simple lack of IT awareness.

'Jamie' and his team of 6 share a good quality printer. They all regularly print documents to send out to externally to customers and internally to other departments.

External customers need to receive; well presented, headed letters on quality paper. Internal staff and management don't.

This is what tends to happen at present

When 'Jamie' prepares a letter to a customer on his PC, he gets up from his seat and says "Printing" to the rest of his team. This will of course break the concentration of the rest of the team who will all have stopped work for that split second.

He opens the printer tray and puts in one sheet of headed paper, then walks back to his desk and presses the print key. He then walks back to the printer and retrieves the printed document (as long as no-one has misheard and printed their own in the meantime).

Not only has all his walking to the printer and back caused a hole in the carpet, any misprints or extra paper from the printer will be left on the side.

Imagine the number of times each day where misprints happen, the amount of time Jamie spends walking backwards and forwards to the printer each day. Multiple it by 6 (the number of people in his team) and then by 5 to give the time spent each week by the team. (Don't forget to add on the "frustration" factor also).

Then work out how much it would cost to spend an hour or so setting up each PC to print on headed paper from Bin 1 and plain paper from Bin 2 and see which is the least.

(Clue – it's probably likely to be the second one).

The printer can be a problem by itself, with paper jamming and lack of ink, especially in older versions. The latest laser printers can be faster and more accurate in their printing but none of these things matter if the content of what is being printed is not up to scratch in the first place.

Although being able to use the printer 'Jamie' and the team may never have had any formal training in 'word' or other software. So when someone accidentally alters the margins or the line spacing in the original document, no one will know how to fix it. As a result, documents risk being sent out to customers that look slovenly and not professional.

And here is my next big tip for managers "Don't design in word"!
If you are a manager and you have a service to promote or market, don't do the design work in "word" or by yourself.

I will say this again – do not do design work yourself using "word"

The reasons for this are;
1 It will look really naff.
2. You have much more important things to do.

3. If you are like most "word" users, you will only know how to use 2% of the application.

Instead, ask a person (in house) who can operate the Mac or who has; 'Indesign', 'Photoshop' or 'illustrator' on their PC, chat them up and take along a sample of the stationary/ leaflet you are looking to change with biro written all over it, to help them understand the changes.

Most council graphic designers will jump at the chance to do something other than the corporate newspaper or invitations to the Mayors open day.

While we are talking about design and layout, here are a few more tips;

1. If there is a 'typing pool' you should find out how to use them. They will probably be called "Directorate Administration Team" or something but they will be able to use than 2% of 'word' (they will also be able to advise on business grammar and spelling).
2. The Dyslexia Society recommends using 'Tahoma' or 'Verdana' fonts because they are easier for dyslexic and poor sighted people to read (take their free advice).
3. Your favourite part of 'word' should be the 'spell checker'. Imagine wearing out the screen where the dictionary icon is located. (Generally you won't 'spell check' your documents until you send an email to your own and to other departments which

means you look a bit inept when they see your spelling mistakes).

PowerPoint and presentations
This is another part of IT and software which seems so effective and easy to use but which can be your worst enemy.

Take PowerPoint for example (or any visual presentation software) – Microsoft makes it very easy to use PowerPoint. Note – this is not the same as making a good presentation...

Leaving aside the "death by PowerPoint" debate – good presentations are ones where you leave the presentation having written all over the handouts. This is because the presenter used PowerPoint to stop themselves from drying up – almost a prompt. Speaking 'off the cuff' meaning that you have had to take notes and listen to what has been said.

I have lost count of the number of times I have been to presentations (government departments are the worst culprits) where the slides are developed in an incredibly boring way or the presenter will have read the slides as written, to the audience.
These presentations will have usually ended with "Any questions?"

And if there are any, they are met with answers such as:
"We don't know – leave me your number and I'll get back to you" or

"We are still working on that"

It would have been much better to just email a word document and save everyone the trouble of actually having to attend.

Here are some tips when using PowerPoint slides;

Forget the clipart library provided by Microsoft. They look naff and everyone will have seen them before. Choose high quality photographs instead. If you don't know where to find them for free – email me & I will give you some of my links.

Don't go mad on the animation & transitions. If you are relying on the animation for your "wow" factor – then you are a lousy presenter. You will most likely get it wrong, things will appear at the wrong time and you will generally look like an amateur. Just choose a striking background and stick to it.

Be careful with sound clips. Not everyone will be able to hear them. One site I worked at, the presenter used the machine gun sound clip to gain the attention of the audience. (Some of whom were elderly members of the council, and had served in various wars and most definitely did not see the funny side).

Using Excel
Excel is part of the standard office install. Most people know how to use it to arrange nights out and

account for money in a world cup sweepstake or whatever but little else.

Like most applications it really is a clever bit of kit and most users only scratch the surface of using it.

I have even seen staff printing an excel file onto a sheet of paper and then manually COUNTING by hand the number of records meeting certain criteria (all records aged over 65 years of age or whatever). This is not using either the technology or the people, to their best potential.

(You do know how to use the =COUNTIF function don't you?)

Always keep a close eye on version control because as soon as you get multiple versions of the same document, you are doomed.

Most databases will export data to .csv format for further analysis– you do know the difference between that and standard excel format (don't you?)

Memory sticks (Flash Drives)
At the time of the events in this book, memory sticks were relatively new. For those who don't know what a memory stick is; they are small easy fitting devices (they can be hung from a key ring), which can be plugged into most computers. The computer 'sees' the device as a drive and you can copy files from the PC onto the memory stick, plug it into another computers and open the files.

In recent years the capacity of these 'sticks' has increased. Previously they could only store a few documents/spreadsheets, now they are able to hold video as well as a plethora of files and documents.

These memory sticks, while being helpful in moving data, can also be a massive risk to the security of both individual computers and the loss or misappropriation of information.

The bottom line is that I would not allow them to be used at all, if I were to return to office management. I feel that they foster a casual attitude to the transfer of data.

Staff can easily slip them into their pockets (purposefully or accidentally), take them home, use them on the family PC, which may or may not have a virus on it, bring it back to the office and Hey Presto!, a couple of hours work has been created for the PC support technicians.

In a couple of placements, apart from the regular work information needed to do the job, I have seen staff uploading jokes, photographs and funny articles from a variety of devices including cameras and mobile phones which have then been emailed around the office.

These things not only cause a distraction for the workforce but can be a security risk and because of

this I would in fact go further than just not allowing their use and actually ban them
I would have all input devices on the staff PCs removed, including CD/DVD and USB drives.

Document imaging systems
Taking a step up from the standard desktop applications, most local authorities have some form of document imaging system to manage their workflow.
What's a document imaging system? I hear you say!

Well let me explain: - to process a housing benefit claim, a customer needs to provide various supporting evidence to accompany that claim.

Some of this information can be rolled forward from a previous claim e.g. National Insurance number (because it never changes) and some will need to be updated on a regular basis e.g. Wage slips

In the 'olden days' all this information would be gathered together in a cardboard folder by the post clerk and the folder would be moved around as the claim was processed. At any one time, a claim (folder) could be in the incoming post section, the pending further information section, and the ready to process section or the process complete and ready to file away section or actually filed away as complete.

Multiply this by 10 to 100 or even a 1,000 claims, pending or ready to process and you can see how a form could get lost in paperwork.

Some poor member of the council staff had the sole job of stamping incoming post, sorting it, looking up the file and putting it all together. This was and in some cases still is, an incredibly labour intensive not to mention extremely boring thing to do. The opportunity for job satisfaction and advancement was almost none.

Document imaging systems made their debut at around the same time as Windows and pc systems generally started to become server based. Initially (like Windows!) they were clunky, slow and unreliable.

But as clunky as they were they helped improve work flow
Instead of hunting round for pieces of paper, a document came through the post, the date was stamped on it, then scanned onto, what looked to the untrained eye like, a big photocopier connected to a PC.

The software kicked in and instead of a person trudging around looking for files, the software looked at the document type and sent it to a 'virtual' tray which linked that document with similar documents relevant to that claim and 'bobs your uncle.'

Being a consultant of very little brain I am big into workflow because it helps get around jargon and manufacturer 'fixes' to cut to the issues.

The role of the scanner (usually the Post clerk) was essential. They had the power to derail the whole process, by giving the scanned file the wrong index name (intentionally or not), which would mean that the document went to the wrong (virtual) tray or wrong person.

Of all the staff the scanners were usually paid the least as it was seen 'as an 'easy' job

It was made difficult and complicated because most authorities had too many document types and work trays and what should have been a job which could be covered by a student/temp or other casual workers, supervised by a chargehand/overseer had been constructed into a skilled job.

I have seen minutes of meetings where managers met to discuss how many new trays to set up, what to call them and how many new document types to set up.

After managers had finished shuffling the 'deck chairs on the titanic', the knowledge needed by staff to correctly allocate a document was massive and the chance of wrongly-scanning by a new staff member (or an experienced one) was quite high and sending a document to the wrong place, caused multiple problems down the line.

What had been created was a single critical point of failure.

Unfortunately, software manufacturers don't particularly help here. Most systems have endless document systems and features which make the application harder to learn.

There were often signs, on all the sites where I worked, that the place was at risk of suffering severe workflow problems and at one place in particular they had their 2 scanners off at the same time as pre-booked holidays and medical appointments clashed

Instead of a job that anyone could slot into after a couple of hours training (health and safety awareness etc.) a beast had been invented which punched very much above its weight.

That's the fundamental aspect of my approach. Most authorities use scanning as an end in its self rather than seeing it as a tool to solve a problem. Whole meetings can be devoted to how many new trays should be set up and what to call them.

By 2006/2007 IT was much more reliable. The clunky scanners from the days of windows '98 were no more.

Slick software can now; run reports, sort things into order and find exceptions, much faster than humans ever will. It's the computers job and they are good at it.

Unfortunately, managers seem to still have trouble catching up...

Consultant as a crutch

It might surprise you to hear this, but chief executives, Directors, Heads of service and some managers may not know everything they are supposed to know and in some cases can be quite inept in the performance of their duties.

This information is of use to an interim because they can, sometimes, be used as a crutch to help prevent the client or director from making a mistake in judgment or for taking the responsibility if things go wrong. It is important for the consultant to be self aware – to prevent personal disaster later down the track.

I had been called in as an interim manager as part cover for a manager who was off on long term sickness.

The view of staff about him was that he was a very nice person. He went out with them for a drink on Friday lunch times, he helped organize 'children in need' events and five-a-side football, he was well respected throughout the rest of the council but ultimately he was not standing up for his service or the staff.

I pointed out during a team meeting that it seemed that we were helping other departments achieve their business objectives at the expense of our own. "We know!" chorused the staff "But we can't seem to get anyone to listen."

The staff were frustrated customers were dissatisfied, they knew they didn't have the resources to do a good job (training and actual staffing levels were very low and customers were dissatisfied). But every grievance or complaint had been met with just an ultra nice response from the manager

Learning Point - Being friends with staff doesn't necessarily make you a good manager...

Anyway, long story short, after a couple of months, I had made progress. I had got the staff on board, and got a training plan in place.

I had taken control of the place by the scruff of the neck and everyone was feeling better about coming to work. But the thing I couldn't shake off was the underlying fear of the return of the permanent manager. The staff were not fools and they knew I had been piloted in to fix things and although this "Indian summer" was pleasant, they knew it was not sustainable.

I found that I couldn't control the actions of the Director and he seemed to have an inability to grasp what was required for the business at an operational level. (Remember what I said about what I expect from a Director?)

I impressed to him that returning the incumbent to the workplace would undo much of what I had done and would certainly shatter the confidence of staff. Finally, after being backed in a corner, he agreed to issue a directive to them.

The end result was a cryptically worded email to all the staff about "certain issues to resolve" which was sent on the Friday at 4:55pm (just as I was battling with the motorway and knew nothing about it) knowing that he would be away the following week.

The first thing I faced on Monday morning was a stream of people who had printed the email off and came to my desk waving it.
(As an aside, people tend to think that printing an email off makes it more serious).

Of course, I had no answers; I was not informed about the long term strategy for the service. But I was left holding the baby. I hate having to shrug my shoulders (unfortunately, it seems that is all some managers can do.)

The basic contents of the email were something along the lines of "look I know that you are worried but the news is that there is no news - more news to follow"

There was no; "I have noted the progress made and thanks to you all", no; "transfer through a difficult time" - just a long holding email with no Director around to deal with the fall out.

Small groups of staff began congregating and chattering about the impending doom. (But more to the point, they were not doing what they should have been doing).

In my opinion the director acted badly and should really have taken some advice from the management guru Gerry 'Robinson who says,

"Shit happens only once" and you should be there in person to deal with it.

OK, so this wasn't really shit in the sense of redundancies but it was stopping staff working and creating a 'feel bad' factor of unease.

So what would I have done?

I would have given a brief presentation to staff (phones covered by somebody else's team, team leaders to telephone the inevitable job share absentees within the hour), thanking them for their efforts, and outlining the timetable of events and then offered to answer questions there and then.

The Result – would have been no "death by a thousand gossip conversations" and more focus on the job in hand.
But of course I was only the interim and it wasn't my problem.

What could have become a problem however happened when I was working on a project which required the drawing up of detailed procedures on how to run reports on a system.

These procedures were important as they were included in the job description of a fairly new and dedicated member of staff and he needed to know them

After talking with the young man and sorting out any problems he had with the procedures I wrote the details out for him to refer to, walked him through them and it seemed to me that he was perfectly capable to do the job.

I reported this to the Director and suggested that this young officer do the job (under my supervision).
"No, you do it." was the Directors' reply.
"But here are the procedures I've written them down because you've never had them before."
"No, you just do it".
"OK, but he is perfectly capable".
"No you just do it for a few more weeks"

This director did not have confidence in the performance of his staff as he did not know them or trust them to deliver.

Having been around local Government for a long time and I know that "a few more weeks" can turn into month and even years so when did the director actually think that I was supposed to leave?

Cleaning up mess

Apart from being heavily relied on or used, by the client an interim is always required to clean up other people's mess (metaphorically speaking). There are many reasons why the section involved needs tidying up but at this place it was because the in-house manager has been moved to another job within the organisation not having had the physical time or certain skills to do the task.

Along with the general dynamics of the place, it was difficult to work out who were team leaders and who was staff.

The previous manager had done some recruitment from internal applicants, for a Team Leader and unfortunately couldn't decide on the successful candidate:
There were two candidates to choose from;

The first was a mature person with quite a spiky personality. Technically very good, but hard to get

along with, she was unpopular with other staff and involved in general 'troublemaking' (regularly going to see senior management about service issues).
The second was a younger person, not quite as good technically, but with a better relationship with the rest of the staff and more of a team player she was "perky" rather than "spiky".

The previous manager had been unable to decide between them and had given them both a six month trial.

All the paperwork dealing with the recruitment process was missing.
Bearing in mind that this would make quite a difference in pay to one of them, what was I to do?

Each of the individuals had a letter from the organisation, with details of the arrangement; this had been signed by the manager, who was now off sick.
The only thing to do was stick to the arrangement that they had been told and make a decision based on the criteria of the 6 month trial.
The irony was that one of them had already been doing the job for a period of six months before the recruitment process took place

The final result was that she was given the job and the mess had been wiped up.

Problem processes

So after finding out the problems from the information I had gathered, my tactic was to get staff on side. That is; on the side of change for the better.

Quite often staff knew about the inefficiencies in the business but they either couldn't or were not able to do anything to improve the situation. I found that I could gain kudos by scrapping some of the procedures and trying something – anything – to make things better. Sometimes it's the system that's wrong.

I mention this because - if ideas were encouraged and promoted and members of staff were allowed to give vent to their ideas, 99 of them might be silly but that 100th might just save the department thousands of pounds.

I would say to them, "I don't have the monopoly on bright ideas, you do the job not me, you will continue to do the job after I have left so it makes sense for you to design the solution not me". Then we would have a brain storming session guided by what I had learned.

It was an eye opener to find out that for many staff this was the first time they had ever been asked what they thought and what they would like.

All this may sounds a bit like it was a walk in the park but in some situations the brainstorming sessions were not to encourage change or solve a wonky procedure but to prevent a more obvious problem of 'all out war' between teams of staff.

In this particular place I was bombarded with queries and general moans and groans about one particular team.

They were the 'Millwall' of the office, nobody seemed to like them.

The team in particular knew they were crap but they didn't care!

More importantly, the team was responsible for a key "performance indicator" so I decided to act.

I called a meeting away from the usual workplace and armed myself with; large sheets of flip chart paper, marker pens and blue tack, then feeling like a real life 'David Brent' I went to the meeting determined to bottom the teams' problems, and get them back on track with the job they should have been doing and the rest of the staff who were moaning about them.

Building a process map

I used the classic process map of a "brain storming" exercise to find out what each group of staff thought were the reasons for the problems (and I was glad I did).

For those who don't know - process map (brain storming) begins with getting the delegates from the same work team or department (in my case - 'Millwall') to write down the answer to this question.

"If you were asked (in a pub or wherever) what you did for a job, what would you say? -use no more than 10 words"

It's likely that some smart-asses would decide to argue about which pub they might be in, so be ready to substitute the question for something like,
 'What do you think your team is supposed to do?"

You will probably get a few random answers but most should agree on the general gist.

At the top of your first flip chart page write the heading "Mega Process" (this is what the service is aiming to do)

Underneath write the 4-5 sub-processes:- very general headings which summarise HOW the objective of the service is achieved.

In this example for a benefit claim, they are likely to be

1. Gather information from customer
2. Verify information
3. Process claim on computer system

4. Issue notification letter to customer

Keep on asking further sub process questions for each process above it until you get to the very bottom.

So in the example above, what are the problems involved with sub process1

Gathering information – is made difficult because of bad form design.
-Which in turn makes it difficult for customers to understand what they can and can't claim?
-because they don't know how to fill it in properly
-and turn up without the necessary information because they have received bad advice by customer services team and other advisors over the phone

Keep on branching out. Just like a tree, some branches will be small and others will go on or off at tangents.

To keep the discussion flowing you need to ask for any 'problems' associated with each process e.g. Take on claim form and verify customer details - you can't do this if there is no guidance on how to do it.

Most problems will come from relationships with other teams or individuals and if all this can be written on a pink (for problem) post-it-note then all the better.

Be very strict at this point as some team members will want to unload and go off into a rant. It helps if you can have another manager or "trusted" staff member in the audience to help keep the discussion on track.

You will know when you have exhausted the problem phase as similar problems will start to resurface and people repeat themselves.
This usually takes about an hour. This would be a good time for a break.

On return you start "Solution Mode"
If anyone returns to the problems they mentioned before they need to be snapped back out of it quickly.

Solutions will mainly consist of something like - the writing of procedures.

At the end of the solution mode you will be quite tired so you might like to schedule the workshop to go up to lunch time so that people who are not motivated to carry on gas bagging.

And there you have your ready made action plan. You will have a large sheet of flip chart paper covered in post-it notes.

Problem People

Having crashed into and sorted out some of the problems of procedures, processes and general annoyances with the staff I could now start working on what could be called the second part of the consultancy cycle and that was crashing into people.

After being there for a while, it was possible to get to know who the problem people were and for some it is likely that even now they will still be causing problems.
These individuals would always, when told "You are not doing your job properly." whine and give some excuse - "yes but, this, that and the other" for not having done it right.

With some of these individuals it was possible to spend time with them, telling them what to do and how to do it, only to have them come up to me and ask me about it once again. Then I would say "Don't you remember we have already fixed it"

They would reply "Yes but, X Y and Z ".

Eventually I had to start making decisions about disciplinary action in conjunction with the internal managers.

These problem people might have been there years just plodding along, no questions asked, pay packet collected and it often took an external person looking at them with a 'new set of eyes' as well as have the conviction, to force disciplinary action through.

A successful organisation?

Developing a successful organisation is about many things but in the main it can be narrowed down to a few broad headings

- Trained staff, knowing what they are doing
- Everyone heading in the same direction
- Eliminating wasted time spent on non productive matters

It sounds easy, but for many organisations these things are made impossible because of the blame centric culture in which we live. When things go wrong everything has to be someone else's fault and suddenly a working team becomes working individuals. "I didn't do it", "it wasn't me"

Don't believe me? - listen carefully at the TV news and to the language the interviewer uses with almost any guest (especially after some sort of disaster). They will constantly pick away at the guest or expert, looking for evidence of wrong doing somewhere – Did the government know about this? Were warning signs ignored? Who was responsible for ordering that last batch of faulty goods?

When a name is given, they are then hunted down, sued and harassed (to death in some cases). No wonder no one wants to take responsibility.

While I was writing this book – the word "blamestorming" was added to the Oxford English

Dictionary. As it sounds, "blamestorming" is a general group discussion (often very lively) solely to apportion blame.

No one is allowed to have an 'accident' anymore, in fact the actual word is no longer being used by professionals – 'incidents' are seen only in their predictability and preventable nature.

As a result, risk taking is socialised out of us from a very early age.
Don't play there, don't do that.

How much risk you allow your staff to take will obviously depend on your industry and its strategies and processes.
Survivor Bias

So why did it take an outsider to come in to shake the place up so much? It was not that (most of) the staff were against the idea of changing things for the better. Quite often their enthusiasm had been crushed.

Most organisations, (local councils and other large public sector organisations are positively the worst culprits) have a tendency to reward "survivor bias' which goes something like this:

Suppose you have a team of 10 people doing the same job. After a time, maybe two or three will leave to work elsewhere. Over the months and years, the remaining seven or eight will be socialised into the ways of the organisation. Risk taking is probably socialised out of them.

When there is a management or supervisory vacancy, maybe three or four from remaining group will apply for the vacancy along with a couple of outsiders, making a field of applicants of about five people.

It is statistically likely that one of those candidates already in the organisation will be successful in their application and thus perpetuate the existing operation of the organisation.

Is creativity crushed and squashed or do you allow staff to contribute suggestions without fear of ridicule?

I have lost count of the number of times that I have come across files with a summary of a case and the decision, followed by the phrase "as per JPS" (my initials) and smile ruefully that it's not 'as per me' (all I did was help the member of staff out) it's actually per the Benefit Regulations but the member of staff concerned never had the backing or confidence in their own decision making and referred it to me.

Historically, in certain organisations whenever something "hit the fan" the 'blame game' started. Instead of making sure that whatever had happened never happened again all the energy was spent on trying to track down the culprit. As a result everyone tried to keep their head down below the parapet to avoid suspicion and thus have a quiet life.

Passing on the blame to someone can often be born out of the induction process of the firm. Learning by "sitting next to Nellie" allows new recruits to pick up any bad habits from their mentor and as in the game of passing the whisper around a group of people which changes with each telling, so the bad habits are passed on. Therefore when the 'investigation' finally gets into the reason for the proverbial "hitting the fan" the original mentors are long gone to other areas or offices and any traces for finding the 'culprit' has been covered.

So how do successful organisations avoid this "blame culture"?
The best managers set up systems to do a task or function (developed with staff input obviously). Systems can include many things, training, procedures, quality control documents etc

So when something fails to happen: - like an order is sent out wrong or wrong advice is given, it is the system that has failed rather than an individual.

Doing it this way, depersonalises the whole thing. Knowing it is the system that is wrong gives managers a chance to work with staff building the type of business that would suit everyone.
Recruiting staff
To break this "survivor bias" cycle – recruiting the right staff – fresh staff with new ideas is essential.

A key thing for any business is recruiting the right people.
Get the right staff and your business will fly.
Get the wrong staff (the problem people) and you will rue the day you ever clapped eyes on them.

I was well into one placement and had diagnosed that staffing levels within this service were relatively poor and there was a big reliance on temps and other agency staff. So it was decided to try to recruit some staff and get eight new recruits who would then make up the full structure for the service.

I remember the Director saying ruefully "Let me guess, you will be telling me you want more staff"

To which I just replied - "No, we just want what we are supposed to have"

Eventually he gave the green light for the vacancies to be filled and I was to get things started.

My rule of thumb with recruitment is to start with the actual day of the interview and work backwards so that timing of advertising, interviews and recruitment can be planned in advance.

So for 8 vacancies that were needed there should have been at least 14 – 16 candidates to interview.

Out of them, it would be fairly certain that 1 or 2 wouldn't turn up on the day and 1 or 2 would be plainly unsuitable. This would give us a smaller choice of candidates to interview and the eight required would come from the 10 – 12 that were left.

Interviewing over 3 days non stop would be mentally challenging and potentially unfair to those seen early in the first day so that was to be taken into account too.

Bearing in mind that the service area I was working in was a 'key performance indicator' for the organisation and I had been given the directive "By any means necessary" directly from the chief executive. I went off to the HR section to begin the process.

I was allocated a HR trainee. This young man was away from the organisation for 2 days per week doing a college course, so I accidentally became the project manager for this recruitment activity. I didn't actually work for the organisation so I saw this as a risk for them because as a stranger to the organisation and its aims and objectives they had to trust me, to use my professionalism in recruiting the right people for them. If I had got it wrong then they would have to start all over again once I had left.

I set about writing an advert for 8 officers.

The possibility that your advertisements, for new staff, will bring in the perfect recruit who fits all the categories in the job description will be extremely rare and it should be accepted that anyone you take on will need training for the position. It's rare to find a benefit officer who is out of work and working on the cheese counter at the local supermarket who might see the advert and come to an interview.

Because of this I would prefer to recruit for a good attitude and potential more than technical skills. You can teach someone the technical skills and the knowledge they will need and it is a lot easier than trying to change their attitude.

My first real contact with the HR trainee was to sort out that he would be responsible to put my advert in the usual newspaper suspects and the corporate website. Which he did!

So far so good

About a week later, large piles of forms started to arrive and when the closing date for any further applications had passed, I had to chase up the trainee so that we could meet and make a short list.

He asked if I would accept an application after the closing date.

Now, call me old fashioned, but that should have bee an HR decision and it was really his call.

When it comes down to working in a legal minefield, 'recruitment' is it and I have always viewed HR as the 'referee' during the recruitment process and him asking me (a contractor) what I thought seemed odd.

A closing date is a closing date and it shouldn't matter what the candidate says - the date would/should have been clearly advertised and therefore applied to all equally.

So for safety's sake I applied all the rules and said "No, reject the application".

I was a bit surprised by the reaction from him. Something along the lines of "it would be a shame to disallow a good application just because it is a day late" and "shouldn't it go into a "reserve" pile in case there aren't enough good ones?" and even – "bend the rules a bit… The council needs to lose it's jobsworth reputation sometime"

I later discovered that the applicant was a personal friend of his and that this was the reason he had grumbled a bit and not made the rejection decision himself.

I felt a bit insulted that he thought he could have pulled the wool over my eyes with such lightweight excuses but, suffice to say, the HR Trainee might not have had an easy night but I slept well.

The next day we got down to doing the short listing.

The way I like to do this is: to pull out some essential criteria written in the job description (the tasks of the job) and the person specification (the skills needed to do these tasks) and match them to what has been written by the applicants on their forms.

I was also interested in attitude and any talents they expressed.

The advert specified – "customer handling skills" and experience in "a numeric environment" in the job description, as the major criteria for any applicants along with less tangible skills such as overcoming challenges and achieving results.

If some one had written on their form - "I previously worked in the …… and had to resolve accounts due with amounts paid"

They would receive 1 point and so on.

Short listing is a very important process and if you rule somebody out at this stage you had better have a good reason, because in these days of openness applicants are entitled to ring up and find out why they didn't get an interview.

We had at least 80 responses and I thought that the best way to handle this was for each of us to complete half the bundle each, then swap to make sure we both looked at all of them and finally compare results, removing and discarding 'No hope' applicants on the way.

The top 10-15 applicants would then be put through to the interview process, with the remaining 'middle' pack discussed in more detail.

But no – The HR trainee insisted that we had half of the pile each, from which we had to come up with 6-8 applicants to go forward. It would apparently be "quicker" that way!

I felt this was stupid!

What if my half had contained all the 'no-hope' applicants, I would still have to find some from my pile to go forward who were probably worse than those who had been rejected from the pile the HR trainee was looking at.

Allowing those who might have been good candidates to be rejected because they were in the wrong pile was just dumb!

This is where I give any apologies to HR and recruitment experts. I recognise the need that there must be some random criteria to cut down the sheer numbers of applicants. But at the time we were not talking about 500/600 candidates there were only eighty and surely time spent on refining at the beginning would have saved time in the long run.

So in the end I told him what I thought, pretty much ignored what he was saying and got on with the job. After all he was only a trainee.

Having got the 10 -12 applicants I set about notifying them of the time and date for an interview and the trainee didn't...

When I checked up on the personnel who would be present at the interviews, the trainee said that he wouldn't and 'sorry' neither could anyone else from HR be there either

Let me tell you, if I went to an interview and there was no one there from personnel or HR to ensure fair play, I would be straight into somebody's ribs. "Who would be there to make sure all candidates got the same questions?"

"Who would be there to referee the interview process"?

Again it was down to me to solve the problem and I did so by asking a team leader (''Mandy'') to be in at the interviews.

Let's face it; interviews are daunting for all concerned. For the candidates, they have the obvious nerves and for the organisation doing the recruiting, it is a chance to get completely the wrong people and be stuck with them for a LONG time.

So, back to the story and all candidates received a letter inviting them to attend an interview on a given date and time.

(Note, I reversed the candidate's surnames and went with the last one first so they were completely randomised).

I advised the candidates to ring and confirm attendance meaning that I would have a chance to exchange a few words with them before the day.

The appointments were scheduled 40 minutes apart as we expected each one to last 15 minutes plus a 10 minute aptitude test plus time for panel comfort and concentration breaks.

In these days of equality and openness, I went with the points system of interviews which is similar to the short listing process and as follows.

For each question, there is a "model answer" with 4 or 5 answers worth 1 point each along with points available (up to 3 or 4) for answers that I hadn't thought of!

So, if the question was

"Tell me some features of a laptop computer"

Candidates would be awarded 1 point for the following

It has a keyboard, screen, track pad instead of mouse, is portable and can be carried around.

'Mandy' and I agreed the following same pattern for all candidates.

Candidates were to be welcomed to the building.

TIP -Send a note to Customer Services if you are recruiting for staff, it is helpful to let the receptionists know what you are doing and when. Candidates probably won't be impressed, after psyching themselves up for the interview, to be met with "what job interview?" by the first person they see

Candidates were to be fetched from reception/waiting room to the interview room – 'Mandy'

Welcome and introductions – Me.

Point out to candidates the nature of the interview process. Confirm that they were in the right interview and understand the job requirements. – Me.

First couple of questions – 'Mandy'

Second couple of questions – Me

Close & confirm decision process – Me

Go through requirements of aptitude test – 'Mandy'. Because we wanted a numerate person but hadn't insisted on Maths O level, we needed to make sure that the person was indeed numerate.

Monitoring the applicant through the 10 minute limit on the test – Me
Return to the room after 10 minutes, putting the test paper in a sealed envelope in the sight of candidate and seeing the candidate off the premises. - 'Mandy'

I have no idea if this was legal or good practice or otherwise but it seemed logical to me and to 'Mandy' – so we did it (after all there was no HR person there).

All this might seem like overkill but don't forget we needed 8 bodies and were doing this for the best part of 2 days, so we needed a stable approach.

When it came to scoring the interviews, we drew up a chart and recorded down the answers to each question. I point per answer, reduced to half where the candidate had to be prompted by either of the panel.

Thankfully, all this worked and we had our top 8 from the 14 or 15 who turned up and I set about ringing them.

I was conscious of ringing the successful candidates as soon as possible and did this from a secure, private location. This was for 2 reasons.

The first: - that it is human nature, after a job interview; to assume the worst. The longer the silence goes on until the call finally comes, you feel it is only because the original candidates didn't accept and/or, you were second choice. Somehow, your faith in the organisation and the "feel good factor" over getting a new job is diminished.

And secondly, ringing from secure location meant that, no one other than the candidate needed to know about the results of the attended interview. It wasn't for me to tell the rest of the office (who were straining their hearing) to try and listen. Of course, the candidates were perfectly free to accept the position or not.

When it came to actually offering the positions, I rang Mr. HR trainee to ask for a template or standard corporate letter to send. He said he could send one but he didn't.

Instead he e-mailed me a copy of an actual letter which had been sent to a successful candidate for a completely different job. The letter included details of car allowance, mobile phone and a proportion of home phone to be paid by the council.

The allowances and phone - none of these things had ever been on the original job description we had been working from.

I rang to enquire was this the wrong letter and do all these things apply, the response from Mr HR was "well you are employing them, it's up to you to decide"

Which was true – but not me personally, it was their organisation.

Anyway, it was a good job I checked because I don't know if sending a letter offering someone a job with all sorts of perks that ultimately don't apply is binding or not. But it makes the organisation look stupid even if it isn't.

Later on, when candidates were starting to accept, I felt it best to track down references and followed up on several that looked a little suspect. Two in particular had delivered good interviews but having followed up on their references and other details they really had not been suitable. Fortunately for the business I had managed to avert a potential disaster. But HR would not have known about that as I had got no help or support from them on that either.

Although for a lot of the time the HR trainee didn't, wouldn't or couldn't, I did feel that he probably learnt a bit more about recruitment working with me, than he was getting from college or even the other HR staff.

So for all HR trainees who happen to be reading, I'm going to give a few more tips here, about what I would do when it comes to recruitment:

If your advertisement does not bring in the right calibre of candidate for your business; remember - everything has a price and if you are offering a low salary – you will get applicants accordingly.

Ditch any advert that doesn't produce quality candidates

If you can't appoint first time, try altering the wording of your advert or even the places where you advertise, remember – testing the changes is the key to getting good responses.

Testing one item at a time will help you track where candidates saw your advert.

You MUST make sure that both the short listing and actual interview has an organised structure.

You MUST keep records and evidence to show why you have done what you have done. I'm no employment lawyer but I would guess that it is much easier to defend what you have done and why, if you have evidence and paperwork.

It's a well kept secret that "people recruit people like themselves."

It's easier to justify to your boss, why you have recruited someone like yourself. Buck the trend; go outside your comfort zone. Get new fresh people with radical ideas. As the cliché goes, if you do what you have always done, you will get what you have always got"

Expenses

Expenses can be a big problem for a busy manager. As this book is written Government expenses are being investigated and the fraudulent claims made by ministers are coming to light. For many this has not come too soon, but if the big boys can do it you can believe that your staff will do whatever they can to supplement their pay.

Whatever you do, never delay dealing with staff expenses, but at the same time, signing things blindly just to get it done will make you seem an easy touch. Calculating each expenses sheet one at a time, by yourself, to check on them, will mean that before long you will be swamped with paper work and staff will feel free to toss, half completed and unbalancing sheets into your 'in basket' knowing that you will sort it out for them.

Here's how to cut down your time spent

When presented with expenses sheets – check a few randomly, then double check them and triple check them. Push them back to the staff members concerned to be reworked for the slightest problem or discrepancy.

This is because
1. Not everyone can add up right first time even with a calculator
2. Not everyone has neat writing (Including me)
3. Not everyone is honest

This will show everyone that you are not a pushover and that you will check what you have been given.

Do not be afraid to ask someone to write the whole thing out again in full, if need be and crossing things out in an aggressive manner makes you look like a stickler to the rules, but this should only be done in moderation.
Insist on high standards – send anything back that has things crossed out or other errors by them.

Then, when you have raised things to your expectations and high standards you can start to sign sheets 'almost' without looking. You only have to double and triple check a couple once in a while for word to get round to do it right.

I tried to get all my staff to the point where they could push anything under my nose and I could sign it because I had taught them and trusted them to do it right.

The staff liked this system because they knew they would get paid promptly and I liked it because I knew it was accurate.

Of course do not be afraid to check some at greater length every once in a while just to keep the staff on their toes.

The alternative (and what most often happens) is that expenses are often used as a way to keep staff under control and in their place.

Running a business or a service where you rely on people spending their own money on work business e.g. transport expenses and then insisting on how and when they can claim it back is a good way to de-motivate people.

Here is an example.

At one particular site where I worked in the south of England, two members of staff had sourced a training course which was funded by central government (meaning it was free – the council just had to pay for them to get there). The downside was that it was to be held at the main DWP Headquarters at Long Benton, just outside Newcastle.

In a car, this would be a round trip of over 500 miles and which meant finding somewhere for at least one overnight stay, to make sure they got the best out of the training.

By train, the fare was £200+ each and they would have to make at least two changes and would still have to find somewhere to stay over night.

These two ladies really wanted to go on the training, but their devotion to duty did not extend to an overnight midweek stay away from home and family responsibilities. So being ingenious (as I had taught them to be), they looked into taking a flight to Newcastle. The budget airlines did a £9.95 single trip ticket. So, for two of them, airfare and taxis, the cost would be £100 maximum. Result. (And I might hasten to add, they researched all this BEFORE coming to see me).

Unfortunately, the wages clerk responsible for expenses pointed out that the policy for of that council was that:

"Expenses for training are restricted to second class rail fair or a mileage rate at the council's standard rate which ever is the lower."

And this is where I get a bit annoyed with "mission statements" and corporate glossy PR & spin. They go on and on about having well trained staff but the truth is that the procedures often actively discourage staff from looking for training & development opportunities.

Because there was no mention of flying and certainly no mention of hotels or taxis in what was 'policy' this meant that, when it came down to it, the training was a non starter, the ladies were disappointed, their enthusiasm curbed and the council's inflexibility was discouraging their input and removing a training possibility.

So I took the bull by the horns and told them to ignore what the wages clerk said and book the plane tickets. Then I got £100 on a petty cash ticket and told them to book the training.

I believe that if I had not intervened, the two ladies concerned would never have looked at or even bothered with any future training or tried to do things by thinking for theirselves.

It was a result – not just for them – but for everyone who wants to move onwards and forwards and not get stuck in the 1980's

Customer service

The thing to get straight in your head right from the start is that customer service is not recognised as a skill in its own right in the UK and certainly not in the case of Local Authorities.

Organisations tend to keep their most experienced staff in an office, away from the customers, as though it is a promotion for them to be given a job away from the 'front line', keeping them safe from the riff raff. Staff at most local authorities I worked at viewed working with the customer/public as the lowest of the low.

But it is important that to be successful, an organisations' most experienced staff should be out in the customer area /arena and paid accordingly.

Staff should be trained so that they can make consistent and fair decisions about the customers needs based on reasoned logic and supported evidence unafraid to make decisions knowing they have management support if questioned.

My initial experience of customer service came from my first job I was a lowly office clerk and my customer service training consisted basically of, "When the phone rings, just answer it". It didn't matter how I answered it, or who was on the phone and for many organisations it still doesn't.

To me customer service should be seen as an essential part of any business and not just, what the Americans call, "smile training".

When members of staff are working at the "help" desk, within the customers "territory" they are there to 'help'.

They should be able to show customers where to go, what to do and not to let them wander around. They should be able to give them the right advice, to serve them politely and not to act like they are doing the public a favour.

The Japanese have a concept which is called 'six sigma' (a management methodology used by successful businesses like the car manufacturer Toyota, First Direct bank and Cranfield School of Management) and it includes something called VOC – the 'voice of the customer'-you find out what the customer wants and give it to them.

In a statutory business like Housing Benefit, what the customer gets is a statutory item (specified by law) but along with that the customer wants to be treated properly with dignity and respect by good, well trained, committed and appreciated staff.

It is of course easier to be polite and respectful when dealing with the customer face to face but when that customer is a faceless voice down the phone line some of these things lapse.

As an interim at a couple of different places, I dabbled in 'Mystery Shopping'

This is used quite a lot when someone wants to test the quality of a service.

The mystery shopper rings or visits and asks simple questions like –
'Do you open on Saturday mornings and what time?'
'Do you have late evening openings?'
'What is your website address and what can I do on there?'
'Do you have a fraud hotline?'

These questions are not set to test or try to catch the officer answering the phone out. – I would mystery shop to find out about the sort of customer service my particular office was giving -but I have listened to recordings of some phone calls made to other services and organisations and, to be quite honest, some of the answers to these questions can be buttock clenching embarrassing;

Employee:"Hello,mynameisJackieyouarethroughtoreceptionwhatnumberwouldyoulike?"
Shopper: "Pardon"
Employee: "Hello, you are through to the council." (A bit slower, thinking – 'this person must be a bit dopey they didn't hear me)
Shopper: "Hello, I'm trying to find out what time you open on Saturdays?"
Employee "I'm not sure I'll just ask" (aside but still audible to customer) "Frank what time do we open on Saturday?"
Frank: (again audible to customer) "8.30 am"
Employee; "8:30 madam"
Shopper: "Can you tell me if you close for lunch?"
Employee: "Erm, I'm sorry, erm, I think so, but Frank's just gone, erm but I think so I don't know for sure sorry. Err. Can I take your number and ring you back when I have found out?"

(Yes, I really did hear a recorded conversation 99% the same as this one).

The result – an outgoing telephone call (item of work) is generated, and potentially ANOTHER incoming call if "Jackie" doesn't ring back when she said she would.

Then there is;
"Good morning, Benefits, Brenda speaking, how can I help you?"

On paper this ticks all the right boxes for customer services but delivered in a very dreary tone hardly inspires the customer that they will receive some help or accurate advice.

Answering the phone is not hard, a friendly greeting and upbeat tone is sufficient.

But that does not mean that you should let just anyone do it.

Ring your own business and ask to speak to yourself. If you do, you will get a very different view of your own phone-in customer service!

Now I would implore any manager reading this to - put the book down, go and print out some A4 sheets with the following information on and pin them to your office walls.

Phone and Fax numbers
Public email addresses
Opening hours
Other most requested phone numbers.

Do it now!

I bet you haven't done it yet have you?

Each phone call is a distraction and the longer it takes to answer, in a sufficiently credible manner to serve the customer, work will suffer.

Many staff have the view that the customer is someone/thing to be got rid of or dealt with as quickly as possible. While it is important to be efficient do not be so efficient that customer service and the skills to handle customers are compromised.

All this leads me on to an event I experienced at one placement where a
customer came in with cheque. Unusually, it wasn't his own cheque he was having problems with; it was in fact one which was payable to his deceased parent.

"This cheque is payable to my dad, here is his death certificate and here is a letter from the solicitor saying that I can have the cash, quick as you can please because I am racking up costs with his funeral etc "

I observed the transaction and saw a copy of both the cheque and the letter being taken.

Then, very efficiently, the cheque went into a work queue.

The customer rang up two weeks later asking effectively "Where's my money?"

Following the case like a homing beacon, I chased it up and got the answer "Oh we have had to cancelled at the bank"
When I asked "Why? When it was in our possession and more importantly made payable to someone we knew for a fact to be dead?"

The answer was "Dunno - WE HAVE ALWAYS DONE IT that way"

Efficient yes but customer service so far down the list, it was on the next page.

And unless staff are empowered to take steps to request changes, it will always remain the same.

Using outreach as a customer service strategy.
I mentioned earlier that meeting people face to face made it easier to give better or even good customer service
We often talk about 'meeting people where they are' and usually it is in the sense of a meeting of minds, empathetically and emotionally, but occasionally
business and certainly local authority staff need to be seen out in the environment they work in and for

"Coming out" can be a very good customer service strategy (but only if it's done right).

One particularly painful experience happened when I was asked to accompany a young lady to a community centre to give a presentation to some elderly people who were unable to visit the central offices.

We set off with only an idea of where we were going and why. My role was strictly that of a chaperone mainly because the young lady had not done anything like it before and wanted someone to go with her. We arrived with our cardboard box containing a few 'appropriate' leaflets that we had scratched together.

We hadn't realized, but on arrival we were told that, there was going to be another guest speaker attending who was from a Government Department. It was obvious, from the moment she walked in, that her role, in that Government Department was to do this type of thing. She arrived with copious resources and literature, a smart uniform and bags of confidence.

The young lady I was accompanying turned to look at me as though she was about to cry and suddenly it was not her doing the presentation; WE were going to do the presentation. WE were not even sure of what WE were going to say (Apparently she had expected and 'prepared' for an 'over the coffee table' type chat with these customers). I jumped in and immediately requested that the Government lady in her smart uniform should speak first.

Fearing the worst I hastily scribbled a few points on a sheet of paper in the hope that it could be used as some sort of 'crib' sheet. Then I half thought about taking over the presentation, but something inside me said not to.

My young lady finally got up and stood in the classic 'fig leaf' position - feet together, hands covering vital organs – a very defensive pose, then proceeded to just read my crib sheet out as written as though it was a shopping list (my hand writing is not as neat as it should be, so she did quite well to do that). This young lady was by no means a public speaker and when she had finished her presentation of 3 – 4 minutes there was a stony silence, only broken by an elderly lady's comment to her friend (and the rest of the room) "I didn't hear a word of that".

Fortunately most of those who attended saw me as a teacher giving his protégé an opportunity.

I later found out that the individual concerned had requested to do something like this for her latest appraisal. "Oh right" I thought since when did staff tell managers what they would like to do.

On return to the office I e-mailed a 'rant' to my manager on the lines of "Disaster averted" (by me) along with a few suggestions such as:

If outreach was going to be included as part of the service marketing toolbox then

- Training in presentation skills should be given to staff concerned.
- Exact details of what was required by the hosts should be known (Presentation, workshop, coffee table chat etc).
- A clear 'script' should be developed so that anyone delivering the talk was "on message".
- A toolbox of current leaflets and material should be available and kept up to date by an office junior...
- Contact details for community centre wardens and caretakers to be kept on file...
- Choosing who should do it is a manager's job not the staff!

As things stood we had spent half a day officer time and half a day consultant time with very little benefit to anyone.

Working for the council

Three types of people & council worker stereotypes
The human brain works by putting things and people into groups. It creates small pigeon holes for storage and easier reference later on. He is a "football supporter", she is an actress and arty.
In keeping with this, I have put together a completely stereotyped guide to the three types of people in the workplace generally.
The first type is very efficient. If you were to say that something 'does not work' they would fix it and if asked to get something they would fetch it

then come back to you and say "I've done that and I've also tidied up our records on this, that or the other"
These are categorised as 'radiator' people. They radiate good feelings and are always easy to get on with.

The second is the type of person who would just cock it up and make it worse.
These can be categorised as 'drains' constantly taking the energy away from the people around them.

We can all be radiators or drains to some extent depending on how we feel, if we are tired, happy or upset, at any time. Usually we can recognise these behaviours and control ourselves in how we act and react to each other in different situations. But on occasions we are confronted with another type of people.

The third category of person is the "serial drain". These are the sort of people who moan and complain ALL the time.
Nothing ever goes right for them, nothing is ever their fault, if they or the department have a success, it was "luck" rather than a combination of skill, hard work, planning etc.
In short, they are a "toxic" person – they poison everyone and everything around them.

Dealing with toxic people in life is relatively simple – you just keep away from them. They are likely to have a whole range of social and personality problems that you haven't got time to get involved in.

But how do you manage them if you are brought in as an interim?

(Bearing in mind, their attitude is likely to stink)

Here are a few tips

Make sure they get EXACTLY THE SAME training opportunities as the rest of the staff. Both you and I know that it is likely to be a waste of time but if they haven't had the same opportunities – and you go down the capability/disciplinary route – you will fall at the first hurdle...

Don't get involved in personal gossiping about the individual. If you work in an open plan office, it is easy to over hear other people gossiping and grumbling. Resist the temptation to offer an opinion.

Quite often people who have worked together for a long time learn to tolerate each other – a bit like ignoring the fact that your partner leaves the top off the toothpaste rather than cause an argument every morning.

Sometimes the tolerant people would say "Jonathan you have only been here a few weeks what are your first thoughts about …..?

Be very careful what you say – they will want you to 'validate' their opinion – you could always reply with the classic phrase "You might think that but I couldn't possibly comment"

Are the 'toxic's' actually breaking the rules? If their jobs involve certain tasks (say performing home visits to customer) do you have a procedure for this? Is it written down and understood by all staff? If not, write one and let them have a look at it for comments. If you just wade in without a procedure and they cock it up, you are likely to come unstuck in any attempts to change them or remove them as; it wasn't their fault, they didn't know!

Does the behaviour mask any problems that you can help with? This is often worth a try, because as an interim you can say "Look, I have no axe to grind, I have no favourites, and I've just been brought in to improve things for you all. Can I help with anything….?

Suppose a person shows challenging behaviour, has a dress sense problem, personal hygiene issues, grumbles and complains all day long. If you go straight ahead and have a go at them, and they say "My unmarried teenage daughter is pregnant, my house is going to get repossessed, my car was broken into last week & my mother in law has cancer and you complain about my shirt not being ironed..."

In most cases 'toxic' people have been allowed to get away with things for a long time and have drifted into roles and responsibilities without too much argument from anyone just to keep the peace.

In one place, a team of four ladies had one member for whom many concessions had been made. Although part of the team, she had been moved sideways into a job dealing with the councils' anti-poverty strategy.
No-one had actually bothered to check on the terms of the strategy and after looking into it, I found out that the strategy had actually been revoked by the council a couple of years earlier.
So not only was this person working for something that was not required by the council there was no budget for it either.
The biggest problem was that it was not a secret it had just been easier to let things continue as they always had - just like in the Jimmy Carter story I told you earlier, I was persistent and did not accept the first answer I was given. The lady was merged back into the 'team' to do a 'proper' job.

Finally, be persistent. When challenged about their performance, toxic people often develop a new found enthusiasm for doing their jobs.

Stereotypes of Local Government people

So, moving on from the three types of people in the workplace generally, here is my completely stereotypical view of the different categories of people working within Local Government which is based for the most part on my own prejudices, although I'm sure there is some truth in it too.

Local government workers do a great job helping vulnerable people in society.

But apart from the local letters page in the paper or gossip columns about faulty street lights etc. all that we generally see of them is when they go on strike and a union spokesperson appears on the T.V.

So what are they really like?

Category one – the Career Council Worker
They have probably worked in the same place since leaving school.
They may be male or female (mostly female) and extremely set in their ways.
For example:
A manager of the painting and decorating section explained (in jest) that some of his workers would almost say
"Up and down painting? No, we only do side to side painting…?"

Or exclaim

"Blue paint? We haven't had training to work with blue paint".

This category of people moan and groan about 'the system', when in reality they are the 'system' and they just don't know it.

Quite often these people can have a strong personal following because of their longevity in the job. They are the "survivors" I spoke of earlier. They are also the most vocal (and often disrespectful) when it comes to criticising the management.

Before you all start ringing me up to say how unfeeling and prejudiced I am - I believe that managers tend to get the staff they deserve.

Draw your own conclusions....

Category Two – Young single people
They probably still live at home and therefore will have few outgoings and be relatively 'well off' as a result.

The biggest problem for the single male is what colour to have when buying his 'Boy racer' car and for the female - what to wear in the office or for a night in town clubbing, so as not to clash with anyone in the office next door.

He is likely to be a 'techie' or may even be a bit 'nerdy' as he works with the computers and probably does the PC support job for the section before the PC support staff are actually called.

She can use the keyboard but her new silk fingernails stop her from using anything but her index finger and her biggest problems in life is usually getting matching shoes, handbag and sunglasses.

They can be both be very useful– coming from school and into their first job is a novelty and they can be moulded into my way of thinking.

Category Three – Sparky Young People
They are bright, smart and intelligent (definitely the ones to get 'on side').
They may have done work experience at the council, or been informed, by friends or relatives, about a vacancy and applied.

They are full of enthusiasm and want to 'make a change'
They can often have their creativity crushed out of them.

Category Four – Mature People
They are often a 'mixed bag'. Some may be working as a hobby to earn pin money, others for extra funds to top up pensions etc.
They can be useful to 'hold down 'functions with the minimum of fuss or can be 'dead wood' and need pulling out.

Category Five – Wasters
They will often have poor health and attendance records.

They are likely to have poor IT skills (and poor everything skills)
They will be a drain on management time and resources. (Pareto's - 80/20 rule has proved itself time and time again with this category…)
They may have been avoided rather than dealt with in the past.

So given this purely biased attitude and simplified view - How can an interim gain some power and implement change?

A favoured tactic of mine was to pick on certain individuals, from the sparky young category or the mature person 'hobby worker' and "talent spot" them, without letting them know of course (duh!).

I'd try to work with and talk to them, perhaps selecting them for a project I was working on, and gradually get them around to my way of thinking, one at a time.
This is obviously not achieved in a short time, sometimes it is a matter of months. Eventually I would hope to get them to go and work with the others and 'sell' my ideas to their colleagues.

The ultimate aim being - to dilute the vociferous workers so that when they say "That's no good, we aren't putting up with that…" there is no one to back them up.

I have been pretty sweeping in my assessment and you might be thinking that I am some sort of tyrant. That's not true.

Anyone can work for me...

One day my investigations led me to the scanning/document image team which had a 17 year old lady as part of the team. She was talking me through what happened on the section and showed me an A4 binder which had copies of all the forms used on the section in it. They were all in clear plastic pouches.

I asked her why she had put it all together like that and she replied

"Well, it's in case any of us are off, so that if someone comes in to cover for us they will have an idea of what we do".

That's the point – anybody could have done that. The fact that an untrained 17 year old could do it proves that.

Dress codes
I suppose I am a bit of a prude and you might think me a bit old fashioned, but in days when the media gets great amounts of mileage out of comparing the shortness of skirts, the depth of cleavage, the overall lack of clothing of female celebrities, and the sloppiness of their male counterparts you might

think it a bit puritanical to be talking about them here.

There are very few places these days that enforce a dress code (except for schools and for work places with safety considerations).

Following the Stockport case, it is not even possible to insist that men wear a tie to work.
For those who don't know -
The Stockport case concerned a young man working, in a non-customer facing role i.e. never saw the public, for the Department of Employment. He took his employers to court because they had insisted that he wear a tie. His argument under the Human Rights Act was that he was treated unequally to the women who regularly came to work in football shirts and other casual clothes. Unsurprisingly he won his case.

Most Borough/local Councils will have a dress code, but in most cases it will not be enforced.

However in the interests of professionalism I would personally insist on some sort of appropriate appearance from both male and female staff.

In the setting of a place of business it would seem, to me, to be inappropriate for ladies to wear very short skirts and to bare their midriffs and tattooed shoulders as much as for men, to turn up in shorts or a t-shirts showing tattooed arms and legs.

If a little old lady came into the office wanting help she would be unlikely to be impressed with being served by someone in jeans and a T– shirt that looked like they had just come in off the street too.

Trendy ideas from America like 'Dress down Friday' when staff can 'let their hair down' at the office is OK as long as it does not interfere with how the public perceive your business. However, in local authority offices, with a high proportion of visitors from older age groups, it is possible that having young ladies dressed as if going to the beach, does not send the right impression.
I know from looking at the high street, especially on a sunny day, British men don't seem to understand 'dressing down' and on a day like' Dress down Friday would either turn up looking; scruffy, wearing football shirts or T-shirts with horrible slogans on, while the women on the other hand would come dressed as would be footballers' wives.

I once worked with a very professional female consultant, who even frowned upon the wearing of flip flops and sandals and although I can see where she is coming from, I think that might be going too far and is probably unenforceable anyway,

Do I care for staff uniform?

Whenever anyone says 'staff uniform' to me, I immediately think of staff in fast food restaurants. On the first day they are given a couple of ill fitting polo shirts and a pair of trousers. Within a couple of weeks, after heat and sweat has taken their toll, the uniform looks as though they have been sleeping in them. I couldn't afford to have my staff look like that!

I do like the approach that is taken by the travel industry which does have to deal with the public on a regular basis.
Staff uniform will either be a polo shirt, fleece and cargo pants, casual business suit – jacket, trousers and shirt set, with smart jacket and dress for the ladies.
All staff will be issued with a couple of sets of each outfit and on any given day you will see staff wearing their own combination of these outfits. They look different, but the same, and smart too.

In many places, apart from the few aberrations, I did find that most of the staff was dressed appropriately and in these cases insisting on a uniform just for the sake of it would have been a bit dumb.
One of the most sensible ideas, from local authorities has been, not to insist that IT support technicians should wear a shirt and tie, but something more suited for crawling about on the floor and plugging or unplugging machinery, would be cargo pant trousers and polo shirts.

So what did I wear to work?
Sometimes I would be suited and booted in a Pierre Cardin shirt, silk tie and cufflinks.

Other times I would be 'smart casual'; soft collared shirt, tie and sports jacket.

I did this is because I wanted say that yes I could be a 'suit' when it was needed but I had a more human side and I was there to help them move boxes/desks about if I had to.

In a world which is becoming increasingly casual, not only in clothing but attitude, the best you can hope for is that your staff (especially when they dealing face to face with the customer), are smart and presentable.

Keeping a distance

A consultant interim must keep their distance from the in-house members of staff. That's not on a personal level but on a professional level.

You are not one of them and you do not work for their organisation. As a consultant/ interim/fact finder you are supposed to get in there diagnose problems give solutions and leave. I learned very early that getting bogged down in day to day things is a good way not to do that.

Being friendly and helpful on one level is OK but employment conditions which apply for holidays, medical, family situations do not apply to you.

For those reasons you need to keep your distance to some extent.

Having said that however whether you are there for a long or a short time you will be interacting with real people and some sort of 'bond' will develop between you and your staff.

This is when you have to put on your 'red shirt'.

If you are old enough to remember the original "Star Trek" with William Shatner, you will know that, whenever the 'Enterprise' explores a "strange new world" the landing party will include not only the stars of the show but certain members of the crew who are expendable. These crew members would wear red shirts (as opposed to the stars' yellow or blue) and of course would be the first to be disintegrated by passing aliens.
No-one cried over their loss and the ones who weren't disintegrated didn't even get there bodies brought back to the ship. Most of the time they were nameless faces.

In large corporations (despite the propaganda), people and staff are often viewed as 'expendable' and although the leaver will be missed by some of their fellow workers, the organisation, as a whole will not miss a beat.

As an interim putting on a "yellow shirt" is a route to certain personal upset with no obvious gain. If you become a member of the 'crew' and get emotionally involved with the staff you will soon be dragged into areas you do not need to work in and

extraction from the situation when it is time to leave will be all the harder.
Wearing a "red shirt" allows a quick, if not graceful, exit.

Because leaving do's can be quite extraordinary. I often wondered why there was so much crying going on at them but once I started to think about it I realised two things: - firstly that there are usually a lot of women in the office (duh) and to be honest women do make stronger bonds between each other than a group of men would and secondly, that however much people talk and moan about how much they hate the job they don't really want to stop doing it. So when they have to, or choose to, leave it's almost a sort of grief as well as relief to go.

As a 'red shirt' wearer I usually managed to maintain my dignity when the time came to leave the placement I had been on.

At some of the sites however I did have a leaving do organised in my honour. Often this was just a quick drink and a bite to eat in a local pub with some of the staff and then I was off home again

At one site however it was given the honour of a full night eating and drinking and merriment and I have to admit that I was quite humbled by this. Married staff had put off family commitments to come out on a midweek event to eat and drink and say goodbye to me.

I guessed I must have done something right in the 11 months I had worked there.

It would be nice to say that I was held in such regard at all of my exits but in the next placement it was a completely different 'kettle of fish'. For the months I had spent at this place I felt I had been pushing the proverbial 'boulder up the hill'
There was no love lost here and on my last day a couple of people came over to wish me well but that was all and I left, job done.

No holiday pay
Quite often people will say something like "It's alright for you; you're getting paid a lot of money". Most times I didn't reply, but if I felt like it or thought it would actually help them I would point out that my fees didn't include holiday pay, sick pay or time off for doctors and dentists etc (and didn't include tax or insurance either

So, do you think I am in favour of Performance Related Pay (PRP)?

PRP is always likely to become a means to an end and further encourage a 'silo' mentality among local government departments.

What do I mean by a 'silo' mentality?
Imagine that an unexploded bomb was being passed around (this can be a metaphor for a potential complaint); the trick is not to be holding it when it

goes off. If my team pass it to yours and you pass it on to another team we can all avoid the hassle.

PRP encourages staff to 'play for themselves' rather than work for the greater goal of the association.

As you can see PRP is not my thing, unless it's done well (which it generally isn't).

Flexi time

If you are not in the business of making components for cars or computers you will possibly have noticed that your staff are not robots or automatons and unfortunately you have to let them, just occasionally, have some sort of break from what they have to do.

Flexitime leave/holidays or sickness all need to be dealt with in the right way..

Unfortunately I have noticed that in so many cases these things, set up for their own good are abused and misused by staff and clumsily administered by managers. However I do believe that with the right management and understanding of what is going on, all businesses might benefit

Flexitime is pretty common in most local authorities and for those of you who don't know what I am talking about, here is a quick thumbnail guide.

The job you do includes having a certain amount of hours in each day to do it. These are called your 'core' or 'target' hours – as famously sung by Dolly Parton "Working nine to five."

Flexi-time allows you to work these hours in such a way as to fit around your particular lifestyle, childcare etc.

How you work these hours is subject to the following criteria especially in Local Authorities.

From when the building opens workers should be at their desks by 10:00a.m. at the latest.

Lunchtimes must be covered by enough staff, if for some reason others take longer breaks. Generally this means half the staff has lunch at 12PM, half at 1PM.

Staff should be back at work for the afternoon (by 2PM)
Staff can leave before the building closes, as long as there is enough staff to cover till closing.

If staff come in early or go home late they can credit their working hours and subject to enough credit each person can take two half days or even a full day off, every flexi period (usually 4 – 6 week blocks).

At the end of the flexi period everyone should be within certain limits of tolerance e.g. not more than 6 hours in credit or 4 hours in debit.

All very well and good you say but this of course is where it all starts to go wrong.
A combination of poor management and staff 'fiddling' can lead to any or all of the following:
1. People regularly going over the 4 hour debit. This means they are getting paid for work they haven't done.
A good manager will put systems in place to monitor this and make sure it doesn't happen.
2. People accruing flexi above the 6 hours.
I have seen 20 -30 hours accrued. This means that a worker has effectively done a week's unpaid work. The department runs the risk of relying on this "unpaid work" and it is likely to cause problems when the person does want or need the time off.
3. "Casual fiddling"
This means that a worker will sit at their desk to eat a sandwich at lunchtime and pretend they are working, and then they "clock out" (start their flexi time from then rather than when they start eating) leave the building and go shopping or whatever. This is often widespread, and I have actually seen people eating a full Chinese meal, eaten out of foil containers for lunch during 'work' time before clocking out
4. Flexi is controlled by some form of clocking in card and it is relatively easy to disrupt this by clocking in and out the wrong number of times or

just forgetting to bring the card to work and filling in a "working" time sheet.

The key thing that most people miss is that almost all flexi time policies state that flexi is at the individual managers' discretion.

I have seen managers sign flexi authorisations slips weeks and even months in advance. How can a manager say with any certainty that the worker will not be needed for work on that day?

During one particular placement, work was heavily backlogged and after observing working practices for a couple of weeks I took the decision to remove flexitime for a period of one month.

Of course this did not make me very popular amongst the staff, but my reasoning was this:

We clearly needed to have 'bums in seats'. This wasn't happening as
50% -70% of the working staff were arriving at 9:30am then leaving again at 4:00p.m.

The Union came to see me, but found they had no argument when I said that the only way to stop stress and minor bouts of sickness was to put plans in place to clear the work which was outstanding

I am not a 'flexi fan' as you may have guessed. I think it encourages staff to 'buck' the system and causes more paperwork for the manager. Where

else, but in the public sector could someone spend an hour to work out why they were missing for 30 minutes?
How much work do they do?

Suppose someone works full time five days a week eight hours a day – that's 40 hours.
The amount of time spent working, doing productive tasks will be much less than 40 because they have to talk to colleagues about work, undergo training deal with corporate or wider issues and then there is the usual general gossiping, checking needless email and catching up with friends.

If we take away all this time it could leave only 35 hours of actual work.

All these things take the same time for anyone who works part time. If they work only half the time of the full time worker this is only 17and a half hours of work from them a week.

Finally you will find that your workers are not as productive at work, as you may think.

That's not to say that I am anti job share or flexible working I think it is the future of work and fortunately many people I've come across working part time [or in some cases full time] spend most of the time when they are at work working out how not to be at work, swapping days with friends and taking leave.

Most managers I've come across feel extremely pressurized by flexible workers and a visit from a would be flexible worker to their office to ask for a switch of days usually results in the switch regardless of them being needed by the service

Why do managers feel pressurised in this way? Maybe some can't say 'No', maybe they 'fear' the equal opportunities 'yellow card' being played, maybe they can't articulate the needs of the service, or maybe they just want to be popular.

Either way saying 'yes' every time someone asks for exceptions is a road leading to trouble.
If I had decided to bend the rules for everyone who asked for flexible working I would have been popular with them but extremely unpopular with the staff that were left on duty, short handed and working a full week.

I would much prefer to work in an environment where I can trust people to work to required hours and when they say to me they are missing 30 minutes I can trust that they are telling me the truth and they can trust me to resolve it quickly.

Following closely behind 'flexi time', in the potential aggravation stakes for the busy manager is, scheduling annual leave. Some Local authorities in particular have a bizarre system which serves purely to generate administrative work.

Based on the concept that everyone is entitled to some sort of holiday/annual leave the organisation will allow a certain amount of days per staff member for this. Usually bookings for those days or weeks will start on either 1st January or the 1st April.
Generally there will be mass take up of leave, for summer holidays, Christmas etc. so who can and who can't, must be managed appropriately and fairly

Some authorities however start 'leave entitlement' the day a person starts the job.

So if for example someone starts on the 20th of October their entitlement will run to 19th October the following year. Of course it will be pro rata – (made with the appropriate fractions in the case of part-timers and job sharers).
Then someone else who starts on 1st June will have their entitlement run to 30th May the following year.
Pretty soon the business will be juggling how many leave days are left for the first staff member for the year and how many are left for the second staff member for that year.

Now imagine multiplying this calculation 10 -15 or even 30 times and you can see that the possibilities for wasted effort and confusion are endless.
In short a system can grow up which is more complicated than the problem you were trying to solve.

If you are involved with annual leave, do yourself a favour and stream line the entire process and sort all leave from either 1st January or the 1st April.

Off sick
Because of job share, flexible working and lifestyle choices, it can take quite a while for the new interim to actually meet all the staff they are to work with. If there are people 'off sick' this is even harder.

'Off sick' can mean that a member of staff is; really very sick and can't come in to work. They are often ill, but can come to work occasionally. They are not really poorly and are taking the day/s off.

You can usually find out who is 'off sick' in the final instance even without meeting them because other staff will invariably talk about them in a resigned manner and a have a 'passive acceptance' that they wont be coming in and they will have to do the jobs the sick person was supposed to do – again!

In most places, I have seen a hierarchy of people, who seem to able to bend the rules and get away with it, develop.
This is usually caused by 2 things;
Firstly the strength of personality of the individual backed up by their 'supporters' from amongst the staff.
Secondly the ability (or not) of in-house managers/HR staff to take decisive action

Before I explain my strategies for dealing with sickness let me first tell you about the problems it can cause.

Studies show that for every ONE day off, caused by sickness, it actually costs 1.7 days of productivity. This is because someone has to cover for them, cancel appointments for them and generally do the job for the missing employee while also trying to do their own job. This in turn generates customer calls and paper work for managers and other staff to handle.

Most places have a "return to work" interview for those who have had long or medium term sickness and this is yet another layer of bureaucracy to bear. Sickness management is a skill which most managers will run a mile to get away from.

Only at year end, when the inspectors are looming, is there a mad rush to make sure sickness monitoring forms are in order and completed correctly.

What does being off sick actually mean?

Being off work due to sickness, means that a person is unable to do their usual job.

How to actually report ones self as sick is defined and can be found (along with other exciting stuff) in an organisations HR policy somewhere usually with the councils' emergency planning document for foot and mouth disease.

Such policies can lapse into custom and practice and only seen to be used by Union officials defending their members

A policy will usually say something like
"The sick person will telephone the line manager an hour before shift is due to start, or as soon as possible after the start time of their shift."

In practice most people will phone in sick after 8.30 am.
Professional skivers will know what time their line manager arrives and will call in early to avoid speaking to them.

It is much easier to get a friend to ring in and then force an awkward conversation with your boss.
The boss probably knows when someone is 'swinging the lead' but doesn't want to confront the friend.

This avoidance tactic has a number of relatives – all equally designed to avoid that awkward conversation:
1. Sending a message with a work colleague, or car share friend.
2. Texting in

3. Getting a spouse to ring in – these are an unknown quantity, as you do not know what their standing is. But that they ring at all, should raise suspicion of work avoidance.

Work colleagues will know how 'sick' a person will be from their own understanding of the person

I have heard something like," Such a body is always off on Thursdays, because they need to take their son/daughter for a medical appointment

This type of thing is a cause of frustration for the other staff in the workplace.

"Can't you do anything about it?" was a moan often directed at me.

My answer to that was yes and I frequently did,

Someone once asked me for time off for sickness so she could look after a sick sibling/relative.
My (short but polite) answer was "But you are not the sick person are you?" to which the obvious answer was "No."

This was not a sick day! It was a day off!

As far as the staff was concerned they didn't get to hear about this or any other quashed excuses because, I wasn't going to tell tales and the person who wasn't sick was not going to share the fact that they had got their comeuppance.

So how do we solve this?
Firstly is the reporting being done correctly, as I said quite often these policies are observed in the breaking rather than in observance

Sending out a policy from 3 or 4 years ago, by email asking people to read it is a waste of time. Most email isn't read apart from request for lottery money and arrangements for nights out.

No, my tactic would be to mention it in a team meeting (again thinking of dealing with difficult people to make sure that they get the same as everyone else)

Point out the effects of sickness on the section overall. Mention any improvements that have been made and how all contributions are welcome.

Talking about statistics and averages per person off sick is likely to make peoples eyes glaze over – so don't

Next (now that everyone has had the same treatment) is the time to pick out certain individuals who have had days of sickness which have been above average and/or those who ring alarm bells.

For long term and serious cases of sickness I would enlist, straight away, the Head of the HR section rather then the normal case officer and try to make an appointment with the top person.

OK so they might palm me off onto a case worker but at least I will have done one of my planned objectives as an interim – which is to make sure that I am noticed and seen to be doing things.

I am more concerned about the things that really hurt a service – odd days, a long weekend etc.

Two things that really help me are:
a. To find details of sickness for the last 12 – 18 months (or when sickness significantly increases) - get a calendar and shade/colour in the days the person was off sick.

I much prefer to see a graphical interpretation which reveals patterns which are easier to read. Suddenly you can see that - the day off after the school holidays, or the 3rd Wednesday of every month appear
This gives me armoury for when you speak to the person. They often do not realise how see-through their activities are, or understand why I went to the trouble of doing it when nobody else ever has
b. To colour the reasons for sickness in different colours – Blue for migraine, red for upset stomach or yellow for a water infection

NOTE: These are also symptoms of stress!

Armed with this information I ask myself if I'm the right person to deal with this problem (dealing with women of child bearing age can be fraught with difficulties).

Usually at this point the person in question might be alerted and will suddenly develop a strange motivation to go and do their job or try really hard way to explain why they were off sick.

Here is a case study to explain the above.

I became aware of an individual who was having repeated days off sick. After speaking to the supervisor of this particular section (who was at her wits end with the individual) it emerged that - the previous year the person had been involved in a car accident, and was trying to claim for compensation through the courts.

The supervisor was aware that the solicitor dealing with the case had advised her not to sue for compensation but after consulting a second solicitor it was suggested that collecting substantiating evidence (time off for sickness) would help further any appeal.

(Why the person would compromise a steady job and income for a few thousand pounds is beyond me)

After an initial chat with this individual, I soon knew the full story, the aftermath
(Solicitor troubles) and the details of the injury caused.

The accident had left the individual with a knee injury which made it painful to walk and get in and out of a car. It was quite ironic that the individuals' job in the section was that of a visiting officer, which needed the ability to drive and to walk from house to house.

With a feeling of superiority from the injured person, that they were incapacitated and unable to do the job that no-one else could possibly do, the individual felt that they had us over a barrel.

So I went into the files and dug out some corporate policy which gave trigger levels for certain things to happen; (which were not exactly as written here, but something like):

    1-10 days off in one year = interview with HR
    3 days off within six months = interview with office manager etc.

The policy recommended that should a person exceed a certain number of days, then all further days should be accompanied with a doctor's note.

This set off the usual howls of protest about the lack of understanding from doctors and difficulties in getting appointments.

Now we were playing handball! I wrote a letter to the individual outlining what needed to be done. In it, I agreed to reimburse the cost of a doctor's note, which would go by cheque DIRECT to the doctor on the production of an invoice.

I did not go and ask the Director for permission to commit £30+ of his budget every couple of weeks because I figured that he was paying me enough to be there and do the job without constantly having to run to him and that £30 wouldn't break the bank. Continual sickness, costs significantly more than £30 every two weeks, to any business.

The result of all this was a miraculous drop in the amount of sickness absences which had been run up by this employee.
Apparently a trip to the doctors was much harder for this person than actually coming to work.

The next step in resolving the problem was a referral to 'Occupational Health' – an independent, neutral person or body (usually a doctor) to adjudicate on the fitness of someone to do a particular job.

I had to send; job descriptions, person specifications and the like, for not only that job the problem person was supposed to be doing, but for other members of the same team, along with the appropriate personal files and sickness records etc.

An appointment with Occupational Health was arranged and as I sat waiting on the day, part of me was hoping that the individual concerned would not turn up. It is a disciplinary offence for non attendance to that sort of meeting and maybe the problem could have been solved by their removal, but she did turn up and the meeting went ahead.

A couple of days after the meeting I received a letter saying that the damage to the persons knee was minimal and

"…the other problems you are clearly experiencing should be dealt with using normal management activity"

In other words the individual had nothing wrong with them that could have prevented them from doing the job they were being paid for so we moved the process up another notch and I scheduled another meeting.

The meeting was a painful one. I presented the calendar with its coloured areas and the individual tried hopelessly to explain the absences it so clearly showed.

I was aware of the individuals spouse because of a previous incident and they had proved to be a foul mouthed and generally unpleasant individual. It wasn't hard to work out that this was a very dysfunctional family and other problems unrelated to work came out in the course of the meeting.

I can't underline enough, how intensely difficult this meeting was and how tactful I had to be. I was a highly paid consultant from a different city and here I was picking over the minutiae of a persons private life.

It would be easy to see me as a power crazed despot. After all I had gone to all this trouble just to get someone to work, but it may surprise you to find that after all the meetings were over I continued to work with the person to form a flexible working pattern from month to month and throughout the year.
The real truth was that the partner had to work shifts, school age children had to be looked after, one of whom needed regular trips to the hospital and the major reason for the days off sick had been to both; help in dealing with the family problems and in the gathering of points for the compensation claim.

So finally it was dealt with and as I have said "What's good for the individual has to be good for the business".
Bash the council
Quite often during low news days or weeks, the popular media will embark on a 'Bash the council' exercise. Stories will emerge of overspending, rises in council tax, breaking news that officials have just come back from a fact finding mission in some far flung country or other.

Whether these stories are true or not, any prolonged media bashing will result in lack of confidence from the public which will lead to a need for the council to do something.

The general rule at that point is to do something about in-house finances – one of the easiest things to actually make, what look like, money saving changes – just to get the media off their backs.

Saving money with financial cutbacks is easy to understand – a winner with the media and public.

For those within the council itself what they get from the cutbacks is not so good.
The result is generally to put a freeze on recruitment and selection (interviews for new staff) and put on hold, any discussions over pay or staff re-grading. These freezes can last up to a year or more.

This obviously makes people very angry and annoyed. Those who had been promised work/job evaluations will find them being told by some faceless accountant that they will be done at some future time.
People, who are promised that extra staff will be brought in to help out, are disappointed as no help will be forthcoming.

The inner sanctum of the chief executive will remain unaffected by policy affairs. Policy managers, Initiative Coordinators etc. rarely leave. They are career paper clip counters. Where the freezes are felt are in the front line services (like umm... Housing benefit) the ones the public actually use that have a high proportion of women with young children, students, temps and other

casual workers. In short, services with high turnover.
All this creates more problems than it solves – because workflow is rarely addressed.

I have often thought about going back into Local government as a benefits manager. Explaining at an interview saying "Give me a year to 15 months and let me use the techniques that I know (all the things you have read in this book) to create a zero tolerance policy towards the slackers and reward good productive staff"

And in my dream, I know I would get; thumbs up, a warm handshake and smiles all-round. But then six months down the line, when one of these freezes takes effect it would be a shrug of the shoulders and palms turned upwards.

Failure Demand & motivation

Failure Demand, (sometimes called failure driven demand), is a phrase that was popularised by local government strategist and sometime advisor to cabinet ministers – John Sedden

Failure Demand can be defined as – a customer demands or requests a service, then the service is not delivered. The organisation has failed to do what they said they would, when they said they would do it. As a result, further demands are made on the service by the customer.

For example – You go into an electrical store and buy a new fridge. You pay £20 extra to have it delivered on Wednesday before 12:00 noon. Wednesday comes and goes and – No fridge.

You contact the store, chasing up progress and they say "We will look into it and call you back."

They don't call back and so you make a complaint, and after your third or even fourth call the fridge finally arrives, along with the delivery people who have no idea what you are talking about and don't seem to care anyway.

The reason "Failure Demand" is, vital, for local authorities to understand and keep an eye on is that, if left untamed, it can cause havoc in the organisation...

Most local authorities (and other business') collect statistics and charts on the number of customers who: call in, ring up or email, the time of day they do it and how long the enquiry takes etc. What they almost universally fail to do is collect the most important facts which are – "Why did the customer make contact in the first place?" and "What are we going to do about it?"

The answers to these questions will of course have to be collated over several weeks to get a fair average. But knowing why someone 'calls in' will allow any, half decent, manager to put together working parties of staff to tackle the issues.

A story borrowed directly from my personal friend (the manufacturing consultant) illustrates why, making sure everyone looks very busy and working harder, isn't the answer.
It is about his assignment to a factory which produced 'flat pack' kitchens and bathrooms etc. Each workstation would do their bit – e.g. drill holes in bits of wood then pass on the item to the next station.

He noticed that everyone was running around dealing with; customer enquiries, solving quality control problems etc. They all looked busy but when he actually measured the work in progress (i.e. the product being made) he found that they could actually have stopped production completely for 9 months, with enough products to keep going for that long. There would be NO effect on sales.

There were so many products lying around that they were virtually sitting on their profit.

It is not so hard to imagine that all those partially completed kitchens and bathrooms could have been a demand or request from a customer in the store yet they were still in the factory and not on their way to the client.

In Local Authority terms this can be seen when everyone in the office is working hard – but all they are really doing is creating next weeks work for some one else to do. Moving things around rather than dealing with them.

So the answer to avoiding Failure Demand is not to get more staff to work much harder but to get the staff you have. to work smarter and more successfully.

The only real way of doing that is to get everyone 'on task' and motivated to succeed.

Many management gurus will go on and on about how to motivate staff. I find it hard to subscribe to any of the 'razzle dazzle' stuff that they expound. In truth if a person really does not want to do something they won't.

I would say to anyone "I cannot motivate you, you can only motivate yourself"

For example; (and a sweeping generalisation I know) but a fat person will not become a thin person unless they want to be one. Everyone knows that (including fat people) if you take in too many calories and do not burn them off you will gain weight. Take the case of Mexico's Manuel Uribe, once the world's most obese man. In 2008 he married his girlfriend, after he decided to lose weight. Up until then he had put on weight refusing help from doctors and ignoring advice about his health he couldn't have been less bothered.. Even when his first wife left him he was not motivated to change his excesses. Only when he found someone he wanted did he do anything about his 560 kg and 'trim' down to 326 kg.

How does this apply to office management?
The busy manager has enough on their plate without taking on the responsibility for motivating someone else to do a thing properly. In an age where people cannot admit to failing in their responsibilities and blaming others, any time spent sorting out the problems caused because people couldn't be bothered is too much time.

I suggest it would be better taking the time and making the effort, to putting systems in place which would allow talented motivated staff to develop and move onwards or upwards and if they leave – all the better for them.

Some managers I have worked with have almost shown fear when they realise that, certain key people might leave the organisation. As a result they have tried to keep them slavishly tied to the job they are doing.

For other workers, the systems put in place will sort them out, almost as a side affect. Over time, they will have greater expectations placed on them which for some will bring out their talents allowing them to move up to replace those key workers who leave and for others they will stay because its easier to carry on as they are maintain the status quo or ultimately they will move out because of the pressures put upon them.

Imagine an office being a pond. The laws of nature state that 'The healthy and successful creatures will rise to the top of the pond and eventually leave the pond to look for a bigger one.' Some may need a little help along the way.

Lower achieving creatures will sink to the bottom and become surrounded by similar creatures. When they join together they become very difficult to lift out of the pond.

I remember that I once gave a list of work to a particularly slovenly individual who looked at it and said "I'll never do all that"

I do believe that the brain takes in what it is told and for that individual the statement. "I'll never do all that" was a fact.

My answer was "I'll tell you what, come back to me at 4 o'clock and tell me why"

When 4 o'clock passed and she didn't come back to me, I went over to her and unsurprisingly she hadn't done it. What she had done, was worked out a lot of excuses.
Is it just me?
Sometimes I do wonder if it is just me that sees the aggravations, the idiocy, the mediocrity and the absolute lunacy of some cases, or is it that I am the

one who is wrong and it's me who really needs help.

I was doing some work with 'visiting officers' - staff who visit customers in their homes.
They told me that they had to spend (what seemed to be an inordinately large amount of) time photocopying 'Street Atlas' pages of so that they could find out where to go for visiting.

To try to cut down the time they were spending and the paper they were wasting I arranged for each of them to have a street Atlas, of their area, to carry around in their cars/briefcases.

A few days later I saw them at the photocopier doing the same thing and distributing them out to each other and then again a couple of days later.
I approached them and said "Sorry to interrupt you but aren't the atlases working out?"
"Oh yes ", was the reply "but we didn't want the books to get damaged so we decided to leave them in the office".
I went away shaking my head.

Photocopying is wasteful in terms of; time, paper, toner, the environment etc.
(Get rid of yours as soon as you can).

It just so happened that beside each desk in that office there was also a sealed First Aid kit, which I had been asked to provide following a Trade Union request for each person in the office. These should have been in their cars as well, but were obviously too new to be used!

Disaster recovery

With so many disastrous people around, I was quite amazed at how little disaster recovery planning there was among local authorities. I'm not talking about the problems in the office now; this is the real thing; storms, terrorism, floods, earthquakes and even strikes can be big problem for a business. Whenever I mentioned planning for these catastrophes, eyes would glaze over (it'll never happen), but the problem is a real one.

Suppose the post office is on strike on the day when benefit cheques have to go out to customers (remember benefit customers include the most vulnerable people in society, and late delivery of cheques can put some in severe hardship) So if, for example - 1000 cheques are not sent out on Tuesday as normal, you can expect nearly two thirds of the phone calls (500-600) made on Wednesday to be complaints.

Disaster recovery or 'emergency planning' doesn't have to be extreme or complicated. In most cases it could just be a guide which says who does what and when, which can be printed off (not kept on the computer in case of disaster) and kept in a safe (but remembered) place where it can be virtually forgotten about until needed.

A short 'how to' guide in disaster recovery

Studies show that 44% of businesses don't reopen after a disaster and 33% go out of business within a year afterwards.

With threats like that, it makes sense to put procedures in place to cope with disasters.

As with most things, a whole science has grown up regarding risk and threat potential but presumably, you would guess that approach is not for me.

Instead, I would like to give you a three stage model to base your planning on. (Obviously I can't be specific for your industry or business type but here are some thought starters...)

1 The problem
Large numbers of staff are not available or can't get to work (for whatever reason).

This could be anything from mass food poisoning following an office night out, to a petrol strike similar to the one that paralysed the UK a few years ago.

Immediate steps
Where do members of staff live? How do they usually get to work? Can you arrange a car sharing rota NOW?

Do it now and file it away somewhere safe.

What do you need to do to deal with customer enquiries?
Can phones be diverted to staff working at home? Can other departments help or is knowledge too specialised? Can you draw up a list of FAQ's (questions that your team is most often asked) now and file that away?
Are any passwords or access codes held by one person only? (As you know it only takes one person to cause a whole system to fail, it is called a "critical point of failure")

2 The problem
"Tools of the trade" are they available? (Staff can or may be available)
By tools of the trade, I mean the things staff need to do their jobs. This usually means IT equipment. It may not be available following a power cut. What safety considerations are needed?
Immediate steps
Make sure safety testing is up to date. Make sure critical data is backed up securely off site.
Hint – have you ever tried restoring from your backed up data? Oops just a test!

3 The problem
The usual workplace is not available (for whatever reason).
This could be because of anything, from a gas leak to a terrorist incident which prevents you from using the workplace.

Immediate steps
Find out: Who is responsible for building safety and security? Where will customers go if the building is unavailable? How will you tell them to do his? Who will do this? Can you use technology? Make sure critical data is backed up off site.

At one site, I implemented a safety test of all electrical items. When the testers had finished, the corridor outside looked like "Joe's Junk yard" with items that had failed the test. Printers, scanners, kettles and even phone chargers belonging to people who had long since left were all piled up – destined for the skip…

Some overall considerations

Who is in charge in case of an incident? And who is their immediate deputy?

When are decisions made & how?

Once you start looking at these questions, others will unfold. Hopefully, this has given you some thoughts to start the process.

To be a 'Chartered Manager'

I have written about the comic nature of some of the managers I have come across on my travels.

One of the first things I did when I was considering leaving full time employment was to go to the Institute of Management (now called the Chartered Management Institute - CMI). I knew that to have a "badge" would be handy for credibility.

In the last few years though, I feel that all the professional institutes have become increasingly commercially focused.

Membership, of quite a few of them, doesn't actually mean much these days, apart from showing that you can afford the membership fee.

In 2004 the CMI introduced a scheme called "Chartered Manager" – the idea was that it would ultimately allow managers to be seen on the same level as a "Chartered Accountant" or a "Chartered Engineer." However, I think that is unlikely – those interest groups are far too good at protecting each other.

The award of the "Chartered Manager'" is not based on collecting points on how many courses you have been on, like the so called Continued Professional Development (CPD) programme – that's just reward by collecting points on a card, but is more connected to the actual work that a manger undertakes.

It is stressed repeatedly that the award is given for more than just doing your job well.

A main plank of the award is that a Chartered Manager must demonstrate "significant business impact" on their organisation.

Candidates are required to provide a case study of work they have done in the last 12-18 months (so no harking back to your student projects…) AND provide people who will testify that you have done what you say you have.

I needed to be a Chartered Manager because it showed (for anyone who wants to look up the definition on Google or wherever) that I had the ability to make a significant, positive, business impact and that not hiring me would have been a really silly thing to do.

The Chartered Manager award is not a one off thing and having got it, it must be kept up to date and relevant. I successfully renewed mine as this book was written.

What I am doing now.

By 2006/7 it seemed that the consultancy 'party' was coming to a close. The jungle drums were telling me that the money was starting to dry up and projects that had been picked up and started, needed to be finished.

The phone stopped ringing with offers to see if I was free and it was clear that being a wandering consultant was not sustainable

Leaving aside the issue of a growing family and going away for 3 or 4 days a week, it was clear that Directors were having to write cheques out for 'real' money (not grant funded) and I knew that my colleague "Steve" had to give almost, a personal guarantee in order to employ a temporary worker in a new placement.

So I began to look around at what else I could do.

Go back into Local Authority work full time (I had 12 years in my previous Local Authority pension). I felt this was a non-starter. My worst fears about Local Authority people had been confirmed and the thought of looking down the barrel of another 20 years just horrified me.

Look for a totally different line of work – working in the private sector scared me silly. The thought of working for some type of 'David Brent' character was not something I looked forward to.

I had heard stories about large corporations, where profits had decreased by 1/3 and the response was that they were losing a third of their staff. To put myself and my family to the whim of some accountants pen, was not what I wanted either.

So the answer was to paddle my own canoe and become self employed.

One thing I had noted was, that at every council I had worked at the training of staff was being approached in the wrong way.
I had noticed that everyone went on the same training courses, including, in some cases, the Head of Service down to the office juniors.

This seemed to me to be a wasteful and useless way to do the job

I have already spoken about 'work flow 'and the designing of systems so that work actually flows through
Quite often part time or job share people would come to work for a couple of days training and never make it to the office, process a claim or see a customer which they were having training for.

So I had this great idea to put training online: - To make it accessible 24 hours a day, 7 days a week, with professional graphics and clear formatting, to reach more individuals and businesses with cheaper but fully effective training and easier assessment of that training.

I commissioned MBA Marketing students from the local university to research the project.

It confirmed that the single biggest problem facing managers and trainers was the evaluation and costs of training their staff. Which I felt validated what I wanted to do.

So Sharp End Training (the company I had set up to invoice and bill consultancy firms and agencies) became an online training company.

Working from our small offices, we are confident that using technology, we can reach anywhere in the world.

We don't use the word "elearning" because people assume that the nerds have landed. The phrase "online training" is one that we target.

You can take a completely free trial of our training courses at

www.learn-for-free.co.uk

Do you get it?

Well I have poured out almost my entire management experience for you and I hope you have enjoyed reading about it and got something from it.

I would just like to leave you with one more thing.

When the consultancy money dried up and councils were spending 'real' (council tax payers) money I spent several months working out what to do.
I saw a job which meant I could be doing a similar thing to what I had been doing. It was local and I decided to apply. Yes the money and responsibility was less but instead of being two hours down the motorway, it had the obvious advantage of being only 10 minutes away.

I applied and was granted an interview.

The interview was in the main Customer services HQ and whilst I was waiting I employed the observation techniques I have told you about in this book.

There was the angry and upset customer at the cashiers' desk, shouting at a glass screen while onlookers stood by a bit bemused. There were the Customer Services Officers in ill fitting uniforms...

Then a couple of young ladies (council workers) walked by each carrying a plate with large cream cakes on it. It was Comic Relief or some such charity day and I suppose they were going to be raffled off to the staff.

Not surprisingly the waiting customers didn't see it like that and snide comments like "easy life" and "It's alright for some" came from various areas of the waiting room.

I was annoyed and a little frustrated because, if those 2 ladies had been working for me there would not have been cream cakes anywhere near the customer waiting area or in any other customer facing part of the building.

Does this make me a look a bit mean?

Not really, I think charity events like 'Comic relief' and others can be a very useful team building activity in the right place. The problem was that whatever public relations or marketing of the service had been done would be undone IN AN INSTANT by the cream cake incident.

When I went into the interview, I mentioned this when the discussion turned to 'attitude to work'. The interviewer (Head of Service – no less) could not see what I was talking about and said "it's in their own time – so I'm not bothered"

Do you see my point?
Or is it just me?

Further reading

Here is a list of books which have influenced my thinking and you may wish to look up.

Management Mumbo Jumbo – A sceptics dictionary – Adrian Furnham
The living dead (switched off, zoned out, The shocking truth about office life) – David Bolchover
Can I change your mind? – Lindsay Camp
Funky business - Kjell Nordstrom and Jonas Ridderstrale
Karaoke Capitalism: Managing for Mankind - Kjell Nordstrom and Jonas Ridderstrale
Leadership – Rudolph Giuliani
Winning! – Clive Woodward
Anything by John Seddon
Anything by Peter Drucker

Printed in Great Britain
by Amazon.co.uk, Ltd.,
Marston Gate.